I0223827

With An Anointed Voice:

The Power of Prayer

With An Anointed Voice:

The Power of Prayer

By

Minister Onedia N. Gage

God's Words

Gethsemane

32 They went to a place called Gethsemane, and Jesus said to his disciples, "Sit
here while I pray." 33 He took Peter, James and John along with him, and he
began to be deeply distressed and troubled. 34 "My soul is overwhelmed with
sorrow to the point of death," he said to them. "Stay here and keep watch."

35 Going a little farther, he fell to the ground and prayed that if possible the
hour might pass from him. 36 *"Abba*, Father," he said, "everything is possible for
you. Take this cup from me. Yet not what I will, but what you will."

37 Then he returned to his disciples and found them sleeping. "Simon," he said to
Peter, "are you asleep? Couldn't you keep watch for one hour? 38 Watch and
pray so that you will not fall into temptation. The spirit is willing, but the flesh is
weak."

39 Once more he went away and prayed the same thing. 40 When he came back,
he again found them sleeping, because their eyes were heavy. They did not
know what to say to him.

41 Returning the third time, he said to them, "Are you still sleeping and resting?
Enough!

Mark 14:32-41a

Dedication

For those who need to learn to pray,
For those who want assurance when they pray,
For those who need encouragement to pray,

I pray for you this day.

Hillary.

Nehemiah.

Other Books by Onedia N. Gage

Are You Ready for 9th Grade . . . Again? A Family's Guide to Success

As We Grow Together Daily Devotional for Expectant Couples

As We Grow Together Prayer Journal for Expectant Couples

The Best 40 Days of My Life: Journey of Spiritual Renewal

The Blue Print: Poetry for the Soul

From Two to One: The Notebook for the Christian Couple

Her Story: The Legacy of Her Fight

In Her Own Words: The Notebook for the Christian Woman

In Purple Ink: Poetry for the Spirit

Living a Whole Life: Sermons which Prompt, Provoke and Promote Life

Love Letters to God from a Teenage Girl

The Measure of a Woman: The Details of Her Soul

The Notebook: For Me, About Me, By Me

The Notebook for the Christian Teen

On This Journey Daily Devotional for Young People

On This Journey Prayer Journal for Young People

One Day More Than We Deserve Daily Devotional for the Growing Christian

One Day More Than We Deserve Prayer Journal for the Growing Christian

Promises, Promises: A Christian Novel

Tools for These Times: Timely Sermons for Uncertain Times

Yielded and Submitted: A Woman's Journey for a Life Dedicated to God Yielded and Submitted: A Woman's Journey for a Life Dedicated to God An Intimate Study

Yielded and Submitted: A Woman's Journey for a Life Dedicated to God Prayers and Journal

Library of Congress

With an Anointed Voice:

The Power of Prayer

Purple Ink, Inc. Press

For Information address:
Purple Ink, Inc.
P O Box 41232
Houston, TX 77241
www.purpleink.net
www.onediagage.com

ISBN:

978-1-939119-45-2

Printed in United States

Dear Father God,

I love You! I know that I do not deserve Your favor, Your grace, Your forgiveness, Your blessings, Your mercy, Your sovereignty, and Your love. I am a pile of filthy rags. I am so far from the original design. I thank You, God for the power of prayer.

I thank You for prayer and all of its benefits. I am certainly thank You for being able to approach Your throne of grace without hesitation. The ability to reach You without any interruption of others. I thank You for Jesus and His unselfish service to us. I am thankful that He gave us some prayer instructions.

I thank You for the Holy Spirit! He who intercedes on my behalf with Your will as a priority for me and my life. I need to spend more time with You and completely consider Your desires and plans for my life.

Thank You for continuing to pour Your works and words in my life. Thank You for giving me the spirit of discernment and the giving nature. I thank You for Your provision for my life and that of Your message.

I thank You for the anointing on my life and for choosing me. I just want to serve You and give to You through the lives You place before me. I want to be a great steward of the talents and gifts You have bestowed on me. May I forever serve You will humility and fervency and zeal!

I ask for forgiveness for the things that stand between You and me. I thank You for the ability to avoid temptation when it arrives.

In Jesus' name I pray!

Amen.

Dear Sister and Brother,

I pray that this finds you well! I am praying for you as you seek a deeper relationship with Christ! I do not know the crossroads of your life at this time, however, I am in a personal storm. At this time of this writing, I am homeless. I am living at my grandmother's house and she is being unwelcoming. I share not to draw your sympathy. I share this to let you know that God has not forgotten about you.

God has not forgotten that I have been unemployed for two years, having financial issues, no longer qualify for unemployment payments, and having trouble getting independent assignments to sustain myself. God is present and holding me together. God is calling me to pay attention to Him during this time. You may be thinking this is easy for me. However, I still pray and meditate and study. I still ask the same questions you do. I have the same concerns that you do.

The difference is that I pray. I wait. I work until something happens. I hope that you will join me in prayer. I pray that you will pray diligently, fervently and graciously until you hear from the Lord our God.

This time which you spend with God in prayer is a time of reflection, healing, and transparency. This is your time to talk to God. There is no one able to interrupt that time or take the attention off of the two of you. Pray with expectancy of the miracle you are asking of God. Pray with the urgency that you need God to understand your situation. Pray with the reverence that God deserves and requires. Pray with your heart open to receive what you ask of God, even though you do not deserve to have what you want (that is what you behave like and what you believe). Pray with a spirit of thanksgiving. Pray like God is waiting to hear from you.

I am praying with you and for you!

In His Service,

Rev. Onedia N. Gage

Table of Contents

With An Anointed Voice:

The Power of Prayer

Prayer Instructions

Matthew 6:5-15 (NIV)

Prayer

5 "And when you pray, do not be like the hypocrites, for they love to pray
standing in the synagogues and on the street corners to be seen by others. Truly I
tell you, they have received their reward in full. 6 But when you pray, go into
your room, close the door and pray to your Father, who is unseen. Then your
Father, who sees what is done in secret, will reward you. 7 And when you pray,
do not keep on babbling like pagans, for they think they will be heard because of
their many words. 8 Do not be like them, for your Father knows what you
need before you ask Him.

9 "This, then, is how you should pray:

"'Our Father in heaven,
hallowed be Your name,
10 Your kingdom come,
Your will be done,
on earth as it is in heaven.
11 Give us today our daily bread.
12 And forgive us our debts,
as we also have forgiven our debtors.
13 And lead us not into temptation,[a]
but deliver us from the evil one.[b]'
14 For if you forgive other people when they sin against you, your heavenly
Father will also forgive you. 15 But if you do not forgive others their sins, your
Father will not forgive your sins.

Father God, how we bless and love You, this day, for Your instructions on prayer. Lord, we thank You for the privilege of prayer. Lord, we thank You for the power of prayer. Lord, we thank You for hearing our prayers. Lord, we thank You for our model of prayer, Jesus Christ. In Your infinite wisdom, we will never be able to understand everything as it happens, but thank You for

Your reveal in Your words and our prayers. Lord, I thank You for this message and how it will penetrate our hearts and minds this day for the better relationship we seek with You. Lord, thank You for the messenger and what You do through me. Lord, thank You for making me the prayer warrior You desire and created to serve You. In Jesus' name I pray, Amen.

PRAYER INSTRUCTIONS

The Lord's Prayer is the most powerful of all prayers. The prayer was the center of instruction from Jesus. This instruction was clear and plain and profound. Jesus knew we would have trouble with the authentic conversation with God so He thought He would enlighten us about the concept of prayer.

In these verses, Jesus outlines for us the components of prayer.

1. Do not pray to be seen.
2. Pray to God in a room, behind a closed door.
3. In secret, God will reward you.
4. Do not go on and on. The multiple, repetitive words do not impress God.
5. Do not lie when you pray. Do not omit anything from God. He already knows what we need.
6. Pray with sincerity.
7. Pray with humility and meekness.

8. Thank God for the essentials of daily bread.
9. Acknowledge God's holiness.
10. Acknowledge that God's will be done. Everywhere.
11. Request to be forgiven for our sins.
12. Request to be able to avoid temptation.

When Jesus determined that need to teach us how to pray, our attention should be arrested. My attention is arrested by Jesus' desire to teach me to pray.

When I consider the elements of prayer, I am overwhelmed. Jesus teaches us to pray in a comprehensive manner.

As Jesus starts to teach, He starts with the actual instructions. Secondly, He shares an actual prayer.

Out of Sight, Not Out of Mind

Prayer is not for show. Your prayer relationship is a private with God. This is not a public display and should be handled that correctly. Please understand that God does not share your prayers with others. You also cannot hear from God if you are out is public putting on a show.

Public prayer is not for God; others are our audience. Public prayer sometimes lacks authenticity. God may not get our whole heart when we are praying before others.

Prayer Instructions

God expects us to be present with Him in a private setting. Further, God designed that time of prayer as a communion with Him. During this time of communion, it evolves into a relationship that is in need of consistent time spent, authentic time spent.

When we pray, we are to commit oneself to a life of prayer, where we surrender our total self to God, willingly, freely, and honestly.

The scripture uses the word 'hypocrite.' The hypocrite is defined as a person who pretends to have virtues, moral, or religious beliefs, and principles that he does not actually possess, especially a person whose actions contradict stated beliefs.

When you are labeled as a hypocrite, there is no trust in what you do or say. There is no truth in that truth. In addition, as a hypocrite, you cannot be trusted with the prayer requests of others.

Of Few Words

Going on and on and on? Is God impressed by the number of words that we pray? Is God impressed by the biggest words that you can use? Is God impressed with the length of your sentences? Is God impressed with the number of His words that you know of? No. No. Not even a little bit. No. Not so much.

God would rather a few authentic, heart-felt words, than all of that show of words without your heart's attachment.

In my words, I am communicating that I adore You, Lord. I am asking You for forgiveness for my wrongdoing and my disdain and my lukewarmness. I am waiting for Your voice to cover me, to whisper to me, to disciple, to discipline me, and to love me. I am waiting to hear You, Lord. I am waiting for You to show me Your will. I am waiting for You to share Your way with me.

When you speak from your heart to me, I am moved and overwhelmed. But I never want You to stop talking to me. When I speak to You from my heart, I am humbled and freed. When I listen, I am made whole. When I listen and pray authentically, I am loved and humbled.

God is not looking for educated prayers. God does not need to know the new words you just learned on dictionary.com.

A Private Place

In this quiet, secret place, is where you can talk to God freely. In this quiet, secret place, God will reward us. Whatever the reward is, God is the Author of that reward. This prayer closet can be your bathroom, your actual closet, or anywhere where interruptions are limited.

In Need Of

Prayer Instructions

God knew us before we were conceived and because of that knowledge, because of the creation of us, God already know what we need. As God has determined what we need, God also decides what we will receive to handle those needs. We do not tell God what we need. We do not approach God demanding that our needs be met on our time schedule.

God has the big glasses on. God sees the full picture: our past, our present, and our future. God knows what is to come in our future, which dictates how God addresses our needs. We do not know that future and how today's requests will effect tomorrow. If we are honest with ourselves, we would openly admit that we used that word 'need' too often and inappropriately. Often when we say need, we really mean want or desire.

I have found that I share my concerns categorically by need, want, and dream then I am better able to understand what happens next. When I am really listening to God, then I also try to seek His guidance for why this was best for me rather than my initial request.

I share my testimony sparingly however, this warrants sharing. I wanted a certain job and I got that job, however, in order to keep that job I had to pass the Series 7 test. As a great test taker, I was certain that I would pass, however, I failed by one percentage point. I was devastated! Fast forward nine months to a nationally tragic event: September 11. If I had passed that test, I would have been in that building at the time of its demise. I did not question

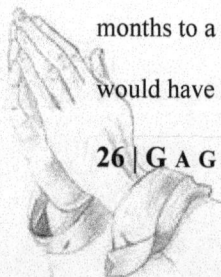

God about failing the test, so when I woke up to this information, I just thanked God about the exhibit of His favor in my life by failing that test.

His plan was much better than my desire to have this new career.

I am certain that God was aware of what I stand in need of because He had already prepared my path back to the original retail management position I initially left in order to pursue the financial services position.

In my finite knowledge, I could not see any of that unfolding until it actually happened. I am glad that I cannot be left to my own devices. I am eternally grateful that some of my plans fail. Conversely, I am glad that blessings that I never anticipated come my way.

Inside of the actual prayer, Jesus is specific. First, He offers praise to God and acknowledges His Holiness. This is not for God but for us. We need to be reminded of His Holiness.

Verse 10 states Your will be done with the likeness of heaven. This is a surrender and submission that we will follow the will of God as He presents. Further, that we will accept it without complaint, modification, or rejection. This is rarely the case—but that is another sermon.

Verse 11 emphasizes thanksgiving as the best part! Today is important because it functions to remind us that He only wants us to focus on today, not yesterday and not tomorrow. Further, we will have what we need today—our daily bread. Even though this prayer should function as a reminder that God plans to meet our need tomorrow, we should insert an apology for the doubt which exists when we erroneously focus on tomorrow.

Verse 12 is when I start to beg. Jesus is modeling this prayer for us. He was not a sinner, therefore this verse was not applicable to Him however, it was all about me and my life. Jesus teaches us forgiveness with a stipulation—a condition. It is fair but difficult. I will be forgiven as I forgive.

In a proportional relationship, that means that if I forgive half then God will forgive half. If I do not forgive, then why should I be forgiven? We want from God what we are not willing to give.

Have you ever considered those persons which are holding a grudge against you? Have you ever considered those persons which you are not forgiving? Is all of that worth sacrificing God's forgiveness? It is not worth it but we decide differently each time we do not forgive theirs.

Verse 13 Jesus is an authority on everything so He completely understands being delivered from the evil one. As a Christian, we need to be able to see the escape when He delivers us from the evil one. Most of the time, we miss the escape route because we are not focused on God. I want the escape route because I do not want to spend more time asking for forgiveness.

Jesus shares with us how to pray because of the value of the relationship prayer provides. Prayer produces the craving for God that we hear others talk about with excitement and zeal.

When we earnestly seek God, we may not follow these instructions because of the governance God has over our hearts, all of these points will be covered.

God cares about what we are concerned about so prayer is how we express those concerns. Prayer is when He talks to us.

I have not prayed the Lord's Prayer in a while and it is still a prayer that moves my heart because of my love for God.

Some Awesome Prayer Instructions!

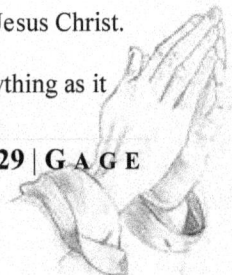

Our Father in heaven, hallowed be Your name, Your kingdom come, Your will be done, on earth as it is in heaven. Give us today our daily bread. And forgive us our debts, as we also have forgiven our debtors. And lead us not into temptation, but deliver us from the evil one. For thine is the kingdom and the power and the power and the glory. Father God, how we bless and love You, this day, for Your instructions on prayer. Lord, we thank You for the privilege of prayer. Lord, we thank You for the power of prayer. Lord, we thank you for hearing our prayers. Lord, we thank You for our model of prayer, Jesus Christ. In Your infinite wisdom, we will never be able to understand everything as it happens, but thank You for Your reveal in Your words and our prayers. Lord, I thank You for this message and how it will penetrate our hearts and minds this day for the better relationship we seek with You. Lord, thank You for the messenger and what You do through me. Lord, thank You for making me the prayer warrior You desire and created to serve You. In Jesus' name I pray, Amen.

The Power of Prayer

Ephesians 3:14-21 (NIV)

A Prayer for the Ephesians

14 For this reason I kneel before the Father, 15 from whom every family[a] in
heaven and on earth derives its name. 16 I pray that out of his glorious riches he
may strengthen you with power through his Spirit in your inner being, 17 so that
Christ may dwell in your hearts through faith. And I pray that you, being
rooted and established in love, 18 may have power, together with all the Lord's
holy people, to grasp how wide and long and high and may be filled to of all the
fullness of God.

20 Now to him who is able to do immeasurably more than all we ask or imagine,
according to his power that is at work within us, 21 to him be glory in the church
and in Christ Jesus throughout all generations, for ever and ever! Amen.

Lord God, we thank You this day for the power of prayer, for what we do through prayer, for the access that prayer provides us, the mutual availability of You and us through prayer, for the all-encompassing, accessible value of prayer. God, we thank You for being able to go to You and share with You what our needs are, what our hopes are, what our dreams are, through the power and the access of prayer, because of Your allowance of us to pray. So Lord God we thank You right now, and we thank You for the messenger and we thank You for the ability to be used for Your work and Your will. Giving me what to speak as an exercise of Your faith in me. So Lord we thank You again, in Your Son Jesus Christ's name and ask His blessings. Amen.

THE POWER OF PRAYER

As I mentioned, these are some of from my favorite verses. I love these scriptures because God gave these words to Paul and Paul penned them with a passion that is unbelievable. I am profoundly taken by the things that this Scripture says. Well, if we use these verses today to impact the power of prayer, I want you to spend time with these verses in your quiet time. Understand that these words are profoundly and positively put together in a fashion that only God could do. This is just a powerful, powerful, powerful prayer.

First of all, God believes in prayer in your life. Our first point is to be knowledgeable of the fact that God can do anything. This prayer reminds us that we have access to God. In spite of all that this prayer provides. This prayer reminds us that we have access to God. Verses 14 through 16: [14] For this reason I kneel before the Father, [15] from whom every family[a] in heaven and on earth derives its name. [16] I pray that out of his glorious riches he may strengthen you with power through his Spirit in your inner being, Paul says in those verses that we have unlimited access to God. We want something from Him. We want Him to know something. All we need to do is go to God in prayer. What is difficult about standing on that power of prayer? The fact that we are going to go to Him, go to Him willingly, go to Him not out of obligation, but out of relationship. Is that access to God important? It is of the utmost importance.

Remember, God can do whatever He wants to do. You can ask Him to do what you want, however, He can do whatever He wants to do, and He could, in fact, limit our access to Him. God could take the access that we have. God could limit us. God could partition our access. He could require us to share, but He did not do any of those things. God offers us access to the Spirit through Himself through prayer. He says to us that it is on an unlimited access when we can do whatever it is that we want to do with that time. Now Jesus, of course in His instructions for praying, teaches us some things that we need to do and should do in that particular time. We want to be sure that we regard every statement with reverence and understand that we have that type of access to God. We have a type of access to God that only God can allow. Nobody can give us that type of access to Him other than Himself. This access to God is for everybody. He did not limit us individually or collectively on how we ought to access Him and who could access Him.

There are times when I just sit and reflect on the power of that access. It is unbelievable to see there are some faiths who have to go to somebody else, pray to them, and then they take your prayer to the Father but what happened is that you have an opportunity to edit it when I say it and I am just in no need of an intercessor. I need to be able to go to God in prayer; go to God completely believing that what I say to God, God already took it without any interruption, without any interpretation of what it is I meant, or without anybody's feedback or what it is that I need or do not need. I do not need an intercessor to take my prayer and edit it so that intercessor can present an edited version of my heart's expression. I need an intercessor that tells God what I said without prejudice.

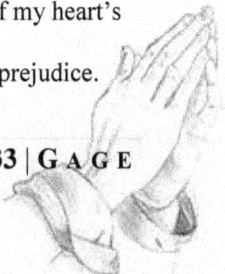

God knows what I want and need. I am only interested in an intercessor that is beneficial to me. As an intercessor, we need to share what is shared with us and not leave anything out. When you seek access to God, you do not have to worry about edits and changes. You can tell God exactly what you want and exactly what you desire. You get exactly the results that God has for you.

In this communion with God, we want to be sure that we understand that access. Now it also means we offer that access to others and we let other people know that as well. Because of that access, we are also empowered to share with others their ability to seek God for themselves. We always encourage others to seek God for themselves. We do not want to be in a position where we do not seek God for ourselves. We want to ensure that we seek God for ourselves and offer the opportunity for others to do the same because people may not know.

Now likewise, there is a mutual availability of God. When we pray, we make ourselves available to God and God makes Himself available to us. Verses 16-18 reads: [16] I pray that out of his glorious riches he may strengthen you with power through his Spirit in your inner being, [17] so that Christ may dwell in your hearts through faith. And I pray that you, being rooted and established in love, [18] may have power, together with all the Lord's holy people, to grasp how wide and long and high and may be filled to of all the fullness of God.

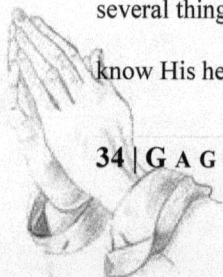

Prayer offers us the availability to God. In that availability, there are several things we need to understand. Number one, when we pray we get to know His heart. When we read His word, we get to know His heart. When we pray, God gets to know our hearts. Beginning to know His heart should direct our hearts closer towards His. When you get to know His heart knowing that we were made in His likeness, it also means that we need to abandon all those things which are unlike Him. We need to share of ourselves with God and understand His will. We need to get ourselves together, and we need to deny ourselves to follow Christ. We have to ask ourselves what we need to do when we pray with that availability to God. First, we need to remember to come honestly. This is a good time to tell God everything. We need to be available to hear from God because there might be some discipline that He wants to this administer during this conversation. We need to come expecting that He is going to share with us with what is on His heart and His mind and what He wants us to do. He might reveal parts of His will to us and what He is expecting. We need to be ready to do just what He said. We should act on His words now—in real time.

We need to be reminded that when this availability of God takes place, there is an expectation that we share God with others. Paul explains the sharing to us in this particular prayer. He is in the position of an intercessor: He did not pray for himself, yet He prayed for us. Paul is telling me why He prayed, and we should be eager to pray as well. He prayed that we started to understand who God is, and prayer makes that available to us. When you are looking for words that Paul prays, he goes to great lengths for you to understand who God is. First of all, God's riches are glorious. He has strengthened us with power in our souls, in our inner being. We pray to strengthen our souls, giving me the power of the Spirit. God makes me aware of the power that I possess. With that particular power, I can do a number of things. One, I can reject my sinful nature. Two, I can share God with others. I am in a position to share God with others in a very honest and open way. I can get in a posture of being able to understand what God wants me to do, but for right now, there are times when I cannot face rejection because I am not strong enough to give of myself in that manner. I am not strong enough in myself to be available even to God, my Creator.

What are we getting out of this when we pray? What are we giving to God? Are we leaving with our whole self? Oftentimes we leave things out of prayer that we should include in our prayer because we are not strong enough to share it. Only God can give us what it is we need. He makes Himself available to us through prayer. He makes Himself available to us through prayer to unmask those things we quite frankly do not address. We do not posture ourselves properly when God makes Himself available. The love God has for us is very crucial; it is very important and because of the level of importance to us, we want to be assured that we give Him the time that we should, what is owed to Him.

And while we may never do what we are exactly designed to do, we have instructions and examples. Jesus and Paul, Hannah and Mary, Elizabeth and John, David, Moses and Abraham are all examples. Noah, Eli and Elisha, Samuel are all examples of prayer warriors. Prayer is a necessity. It's accessibility. It's powerful. It's necessary. It is not going to change because we got here in this new generation. Even if you are not an old Testament Christian, Jesus prays. He prays. Jesus spent hours praying to God telling God exactly what it is that is on His mind. What it is exactly that He wants is a mystery that we should likewise pray, but for Paul to share with us in prayer, it is no mystery. It is no unique incident or activity. It is something that we should expect to do. It is something that we should expect to happen. It is something that should be expected when you consider what is required of us. What is it that we are required as Christians to do? We want to be sure that we share the Bible's requirement of prayer. You would want to pray. Prayer is something that you should want to do. God is waiting to hear from you, and it is something you should want to share with Him.

Now the actual value of prayer is that God makes Himself available and because He is able to make Himself available, we are able to access Him. God is in a position where we can talk to Him and commune with Him and have communion with others. Whatever you put into prayer, you are going to get God's will out. This is not time to thing to do nothing and get everything out that I want to know. No, but this is an encouragement for putting everything in and get everything out that God wants you to have. The actual value weighs on you putting all that you have into a prayer and understand that God is going to share with you and give to you what it is that is His will.

More importantly, I also wanted you to understand that God wants to give you of Himself, even though God gives you of Himself and shares with you who He is and what is that He wants from you, and does so when we do not deserve His attention in this manner. He is going to give you Himself, and because He wants to do so, and because He makes that happen, you have to submit yourself to His will. Prayer is a profound and powerful communication and activity. Prayer is not something that you check the box to say you have completed it. Prayer is a wonderful communication and communion between you and God. Inside of that communication is where you can share who you are, who you hope to become, and what you would like for God to do for you. Inside of that communication, God finally has you at your most vulnerable self. Prayer is a conversation, not a monologue, when you can exhibit your most vulnerable self, share your most vulnerable emotions with God, and put your false self aside. You want to give God the best of yourself. You want to give your best self to God because He wants the best of you. You want that of you and with the time that you give to God in prayer you do not want to miss an opportunity to give God all of you. Prayer is the time to get that done. Prayer is the best time to give God all of you.

Verses 20 and 21 read: [20] Now to him who is able to do immeasurably more than all we ask or think according to his power that is at work within us [21] to him be glory in the church and in Christ Jesus throughout all generations, for ever and ever! Amen. The King James version says: [21] Now unto him that can do exceedingly abundantly more than all we can ask or think. He takes who I am and what I have, and He increases it at an above outstanding level such that I can give him the glory, and that is very important. This is the power of prayer. The power of prayer that restores you. Prayer reinvents you. Prayers reignite you. Prayer returns you to the hands of God. Look at how He blesses you and loves you this day!

Lord God, thank You for this word and the power of prayer. Thank You for being able to posture us in such a fashion that You love us just because and thank You for the allowance of the communication that gives access to the availability of the absolute value of prayer to You. Lord God, we thank You afresh for hearing this message and the action it will cause us to take. Thank You for our prayer life. Lord God, we thank You afresh for Paul and his messages to us. Thank You for His example of intercession. Thank You for him being obedient to You so that we may have him as an example. Lord God, afresh we thank You for Your love that You give us unconditionally, without prejudice, and without judgment at all times. In Your Son Jesus' name, I pray and ask these blessings. Amen.

Time With The Master

John 17:1-5 (NIV)

Jesus Prays to Be Glorified

17 After Jesus said this, he looked toward heaven and prayed: "Father, the hour has come. Glorify your Son, that your Son may glorify you. [2] For you granted him authority over all people that he might give eternal life to all those you have given him.[3] Now this is eternal life: that they know you, the only true God, and Jesus Christ, whom you have sent. [4] I have brought you glory on earth by finishing the work you gave me to do. [5] And now, Father, glorify me in your presence with the glory I had with you before the world began.

Lord God, I thank You afresh for the word that You have for us today. Lord, we thank You right now that You're going to completely fill us with all that You have for us and all that You want us to be. Lord God, we thank You right now for offering us Jesus Christ. Please show us and share with us how exactly You intend for us to spend time with You. Lord God, we thank You right now that You did this before, and now You offer us this lesson and these words. It is in Your Son, Jesus' name that I pray and ask these blessings over Your vessel. Amen.

TIME WITH THE MASTER

Verse one reads: "After Jesus said this, He looked toward heaven and prayed: "Father, the hour has come. Glorify Your Son, that Your Son may glorify You." The opening of this text is that Jesus prayed for Himself. Clearly we have all prayed for ourselves, and there is nothing wrong with that. There is nothing selfish about it. It is just a point where we have prayed for ourselves. In this text and this context, it is approaching the time that He will be crucified, buried and resurrected. Jesus is bringing some closure to His 33 years here on earth, this time that He spent here.

The first thing we want to talk about is on your mind. The way that Jesus expresses Himself to God allows us to understand that God was on His mind as well He should be on ours. We have to reflect and understand that Jesus is going to be with our God and our Father. He is our Christ; He is our friend. He wants us in a particular situation where we can access the Father as well. But is it on your mind? We live busy lives. We lead busy lives. We have families. We have things going on at all times. However, we need to realize that we need to spend time with the Master. In this time that we spend with God, what do we tell Him and what does He want to know? What should we be sharing and when do we do this? We have to give ourselves to Him in an authentic manner. When we give this time to the Master, it is committed time, and nothing else can happen and nothing else can interrupt. Similar to the time when I spend time to prepare these sermons. I cannot have anything else going on. If I have anything else going on, I will be distracted away my purpose, my focus. It is time dedicated and committed just to Him. I mentioned that we lived busy lives, we lead busy lives but when we are going to meetings, we silence our phones. That is part of the meeting norms. Well, as a part of those meeting norms, we can shut our phones off and commit to that meeting for an hour or two hours or however long the meeting is. But can we give that same time to God?

Now understand that we have a position in this situation where we want to make sure that we are praying and we are spending time and studying. We can be able to shut that time off and give Him that time. When I teach bible study classes, I often ask people what kind of time do they spend with God. They give me all these excuses about why they have not and when they have and what happened. I said I was sorry, I understand that we are all busy. I understand that, but the problem I have with being so busy is that we have these talents because of God. We have these things because of God. We have all this stuff because of God, but we cannot make time for God. You have to schedule time with the Master. What time belongs to Him? Unadulterated, uninterrupted time with God. Who does that? And we have to be able to spend time with the Master. We have to be able to consider that this is the time that we need to spend with God. He deserves that, and we should desire it. We should crave that time yet we do not. So when we keep it on our minds that we need to spend this time with Him then we can better manage ourselves. You see, time with the Master gives us time to detox, unwind, share, and calm down.

Time With the Master

I recently had an incident where my car was overheating. My daughter is a worrier and was asking me multiple questions, and one after another. I finally said, "Your anxiety is too much. Calm down." You see I had managed to get us to the meeting where I was scheduled. I wanted to be in a cool place because it is 100 and some odd degrees in Texas at that time, with a restroom, and in a comfortable, safe environment. After I arrived and solved our immediate issues, then I was able to think. I was able to think about what it is that we were doing next. I was able to call a tow truck. I did not want to stop at my initial options, which was the middle of the street, on the side of the road in a residential neighborhood, or somewhere else inconvenient. I did not want to do that. But I had to get there through some duress. You see I had to drive down the street while there is coolant pouring out of my car, and someone saying there's coolant pouring out of your car!

Well, we have to get ourselves to a place where we are not in duress, and we are not having issues getting to God. Even if we are having some difficulties, we press forward to make that time happen. We are not perfect. We are not all consistent all the time, but the goal is to be consistent as much as you possibly can as often as you can because we need to get to a place where the time is important. We have to get to a place where time with the Master happens because that time is important enough for you to make it happen. I want to be able to get to God. Get to Him with a sense of urgency that He deserves. And I have to make that time happen. See God makes time for me. He makes things happen for me. Because He makes those things happen for me, I want to be able to make those same things happen for Him because He deserves that. Again I should crave that time with God where I want to be with Him and He wants to be with me. It needs to be on my mind. Time with Him needs to be a priority for me.

We talk about how we are busy people, and yes we are, but we make time for the things that are important. My pastor has said numerous times that where you spend your money and where you spend your time is where your treasures are. Because of that, we want to be intentional about what we do for God, how we spend that time and keep Him on our minds.

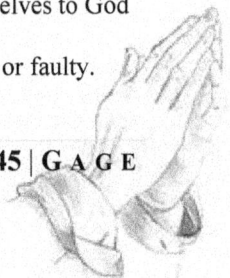

Secondly, when we spend time with the Master, He resides in our hearts. When Christ shares these words with God, you can feel His heart. You can feel His heart! And God granted Jesus authority over all people that He might give eternal life to all those You have given Him. Now this is eternal life that they may know You as the only true God and Jesus Christ whom You have sent. You can feel His heart. You can feel His heart in a very transparent way. And when you feel God's heart like that you want to put yourself in the position where you are able to allow Him to feel your heart as well. I said several times we have to position ourselves better in that we want to give of ourselves to God so that He understands that the creation He made is not fake, false, or faulty.

We want to give Him ourselves in a way that we are just real authentic to Him. In this authenticity, we understand that He is our God and because He is our God, we want to give Him our very best.

Most everyone wants to be in a relationship and they want that relationship to be healthy and whole and something that you want to spend time on and spend time with and you want to give that person your heart. You want to give it without strings attached, without conditions, without holding anything back, giving it your total self, your total immersion. Well, do we do God like that? Do we give God our total self? Most of the time the answer is no. Most of the time the answer is something like, not so much. But we are willing to give the time and treasure to people who we just meet, persons that we do not know that well, people who we are not sure have our best interests in mind but we are too busy to spend time and give our hearts over to God.

We have to change our priority level. What time belongs to Him? What part of your heart does He have? Does He get our leftovers or does He get our first fruits, which is what He commanded of us? Does He get the things that we want or we should give Him? What does He get? You see, we cannot give Him anything and that is raggedy. By nature, that is faulty. We cannot give Him leftovers. Because leftovers never go that well. We cannot give Him something we pieced together with some scraps. That is not ok. What we want to be able to do is give Him our heart. Deuteronomy 6:5 says, "Love the Lord your God with all of your heart with all of your mind and with all of your soul." He loved us enough to create us. He loves us enough to have formed us in our mother's womb. He loved us enough to give up His Son for us. You see, when Deuteronomy says love the Lord your God with all your heart, all your soul and all of your strength, those words call forward the heart and the soul and the strength into action. The soul and strength automatically follow the heart. It is the nature of love which originates in the heart. We need to give Him what is in our hearts. We need to spend time with Him. We are going to give Him the very best. We expect the very best from Him.

We have to give ourselves in this relationship just as if we would to a human being. When we want to go on a date with that new special person, we get there on time, even a few minutes early. We tried on three or four outfits. We groomed our hair. We arch our eyebrows. We have spent hours and money to prepare for a few hours with someone we do not know and want to know better. Do we prepare like that for God? Are we on time? Do we run home and then hurry and rush to spend time with God? Do we say 'oh I wish you all would hurry up' as you drive because I am going to spend time with the Master.

The time gives an indication if our heart is pointed towards God or if it's being distracted towards something else where our heart is pointed towards God and that is it. We have to get to that point. We have got to get our hearts pointed in the right direction, where we want to spend time with the Master where it becomes very important to us and it becomes a priority and where others understand that as well.

I used to exercise regularly, very careful about my body health and people knew my gym schedule. 'You know she goes to the gym at 8 o'clock. You know she goes to the gym at 9 o'clock. You know she goes to the gym at 6 o'clock on Wednesday and you cannot interrupt that time.' But likewise people should know when I meditate so they do not call during my prayer time. They should know when I do those types of things when I spend time with God because they should not interrupt my time that I spend. We have to make God our priority. Time with the master is something that we should cherish and we deserve and we know that we need it.

We need to get into a quiet place with God and share with God the burdens of our heart, the burdens of our soul, the burdens of our mind, the burdens of our spirit and allow Him to speak, telling us exactly how those burdens will be resolved. When you get into a position, a total surrender to God that He understands, that we understand His position and what He does for us. We have to get there. Verses 4 and 5: [4]I have brought you glory on earth by finishing the work you gave me to do. [5]And now, Father, glorify me in your presence with the glory I had with you before the world began.

Time with the Master is evident through our service. Jesus walked this earth for 33 years. He performed miracles. He prayed. He provided. He postured Himself as our leader. He positions us to follow Him. He produced the results for which He was designed. Can we say those things? Can we say those things? Some of us can say that we put off what God has planned for us. Some of us can say that we predict our own failures and God has said differently. Some of us can say that we tried to prove His word wrong by our indignant disobedience. And some of us pressure others to do the things we know we should not do. We pressure others to avoid exactly what we are designed for. We do not encourage them towards producers that God has designed. And we want to avoid that with all that we have and all that we know.

We are designed to do several things. Our service is preordained. Our service is ordered and orchestrated by God. God has given us particular gifts and in those particular gifts, He has given us gifts to give to others. We need to get in a position where we can give ourselves away. There is a song that says 'I give myself away, so You can use me.' You lose nothing by giving of yourself to someone else. None of your resources. None of your resource of time. None of your resources. None of your finances. None of that. All of that can be done. God can use who you are, without you losing a single thing.

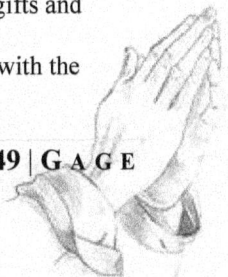

Loving others does not mean you will ever run out of love. Feel free to love and love freely. Give it away. That's what love is designed for—to give it away. Your service to others, serving other people, giving of your gifts and talent—you are not going to run out of service or gifts. Your time with the

Master is going to be evident through your service because the more you serve the more you share then He is priority in your life. Your service allows everyone to understand you are not stingy, that you do not have your hand closed. God sends blessings to whom God can bless through. If He cannot send a blessing through you, it is likely your blessings are going to be limited.

Jesus says in His word: I am here to preach the gospel, I am here to make disciples, I am here to give you the charge to go ye therefore make disciples of all men baptizing them in the name of the Father, the Son, and the Holy Spirit. But when He came and spent time with the twelve, and then by extension the 5000 men, women and children and also fed them, and then those persons who He has helped be free of leprosy, be free of death, be free of the issue of blood, be free of blindness, be free of lameness, Jesus demonstrated how important service is to God. Those persons to whom He has extended His power by showing up at the proper time, doing the right thing is our example of how our service should look.

He never said He did not have time. The disciples tried to keep the children from Him but Jesus says, 'Bring Me those children, that is our generation. They need to understand who I am and why I exist.' He did not shun them or send them off. He never said that He did not have time. He did exactly what His Father said to Him as it says in His word. "I have brought You glory on earth by completing the work that You gave Me to do." Ephesians 2, verses 9 and 10 reads: [9]not by works, so that no one can boast. [10] For we are God's handiwork, created in Christ Jesus to do good works, which God prepared in advance for us to do. It was not something God thought of once Jesus got here.

God knew Jesus' assignment ahead of time. He knew that well in advance. But we are God's workmanship created in Christ Jesus to do good work, which God prepared in advance for us to do. Again Ephesians 2 verse 10. So we cannot say this is happenstance. Jeremiah 29:11 says for I know the plans I have for you. Jeremiah 1:5 says: I knew you before I knitted you in your mother's womb. These plans are not new, whatever you are designed to do did not just come up yesterday in a conversation. It's been the whole plan all along and what we are going to have to do is make sure that our work is representative of that. Our attitude, our heart, our mind are all aligned such that we spend time with the Master. So make time, get in a quiet place, figure it out, and make it a priority. Because He desires to have a word with you and a word that is a profoundly powerful word that is going to produce and promote life within you and therefore you will be contagious to provoke life within others.

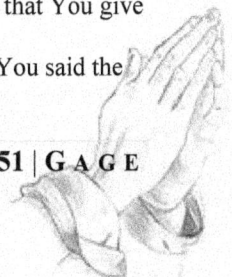

Lord God how we bless You and how we love You for this word this day Lord God. I thank You right now for You have given us exactly what You would have for us to have today Lord God. I thank You right now that You give us Your ultimate power, You have given us Your Son. Lord God, You said the word was with God the word was God in John 1 verses 1 and 2, and because You have given Him to us before the beginning of earth, before the beginning of time, Lord God, we thank You for what He has done on this earth in 33 years which has lasted more than 2000.

Lord, right now we thank You for anointing us, giving us Your life, life through Your word, life through Your message, life through the deeds of others who are around us. We thank You for who serves us and for whom we serve. Lord God, afresh we thank You for forgiving us of our sins, we deserve nothing but You continue to give over and over and over again. Allow us to forgive as You forgive us. And Lord, I thank You for this vessel You have chosen to use. Thank You for my anointing. Thank You for the lives who will be changed and helped by what this word has done today. It is in Your Son Jesus' name we pray. Amen.

A Real Prayer Warrior

John 17:6-19 (NIV)

Jesus Prays for His Disciples

6 “I have revealed you to those whom you gave me out of the world. They were
yours; you gave them to me and they have obeyed your word. 7 Now they know
that everything you have given me comes from you. 8 For I gave them the words
you gave me and they accepted them. They knew with certainty that I came
from you, and they believed that you sent me. 9 I pray for them. I am not praying
for the world, but for those you have given me, for they are yours. 10 All I have
is yours, and all you have is mine. And glory has come to me through them. 11 I
will remain in the world no longer, but they are still in the world, and I am
coming to you. Holy Father, protect them by the power of your name, the name
you gave me, so that they may be one as we are one. 12 While I was with them, I
protected them and kept them safe by that name you gave me. None has been
lost except the one doomed to destruction so that Scripture would be fulfilled.

13 “I am coming to you now, but I say these things while I am still in the world,
so that they may have the full measure of my joy within them. 14 I have given
them your word and the world has hated them, for they are not of the world any
more than I am of the world. 15 My prayer is not that you take them out of the
world but that you protect them from the evil one. 16 They are not of the world,
even as I am not of it. 17 Sanctify them by[d] the truth; your word is truth. 18 As
you sent me into the world, I have sent them into the world. 19 For them I
sanctify myself, that they too may be truly sanctified.

Dear God, afresh we thank You for this day for what You do for us through this word. We thank You right now for the power of intercessory prayer. We thank You right now Lord God that You gave us exactly what we need, that You send people in places for us and to give us what we did ask according to Your will. Right now, Lord God we thank You for this day, this message, this vessel that You will use to glorify You. In the name of Jesus our Savior, we pray and we ask You to bless us. Amen.

A Real Prayer Warrior

The last 14 verses that I read shares how important it is that we understand that Jesus came here in the flesh to fulfill the scripture. God has created us, and we sinned, then He got disgruntled with us, so then God took away all of us by flood and then He modified the world again and sent His Son Jesus Christ. So with all of being said I want to be clear that once we understand how much God loves us that He does the things He does for us yet we still do not do all what we are supposed to do for Him. Therefore, we have to get to a point in our lives that we understand a few things. Jesus' job was to cleanse. We are made whole because of His obedience. We are made whole because He did exactly what He was supposed to do. Because of His obedience, we can do what we are supposed to do.

Now, let us talk about a real prayer warrior. Jesus said several things, first He is our Advocate. Verse 8 and 9 reads: "[8]They knew with certainty that I came from you, and they believed that you sent me. [9] I pray for them. I am not praying for the world, but for those you have given me, for they are yours." Jesus advocates for us to the Father. He goes before God and says to God, they did what they were supposed to do. They gave at the level that You would expect of them. We can do what it is You called Me to do because of You who sent Me.

He advocates again in that the Father protects us by the power of Your name, the name You gave Me, so that they may be one as We are one. He is asking that we have the same privileges that He has and while that is impossible, for the most part, because we are sin stained each in our own way. He does not want us to not have all of what there is to have of life. He wants us to be a part of this God-sized life. Jesus advocates for us. He takes our petitions; He takes who we are before the Father. Jesus takes an interest in us becoming the best representative of God that we can. He wants us to be able to be looked at us better than we really are. He advocates for us. Jesus is our mediator to God. As He advocates for us, just as He give us of himself, He mediates on our behalf to God. He wants to share with God and give us a good report card. He's like having a teacher, you know when you go to school, and your teacher is absent so the teacher leaves a substitute. When Jesus came, He was not a substitute. Jesus is the new teacher, the extension of God. He wanted to report on how we are doing. Jesus even went as far as to say everybody did fine except for the one who had to be the betrayer because of the fulfillment of the scriptures. If he had not had to do that, he might have been alright, do you see it? He takes us before the Father in a very loving way. He loves all of us. He loves us more than what we are worth. He validates and creates a better net worth of our sins.

Today, what we crave is financial net worth. What are you worth? What is your net worth? What do you own that gives you value? But Jesus is not talking about our financial value. He is talking about our character. Who are we? How do we receive our Savior? How do we receive a man who was born to go and die for our sins? How do we receive that person? So how we receive that person, how we receive Him, how we behave, is evidence of our character. We have to behave like the Christians we are designed to be. Sometimes we do not; sometimes we do not behave that way. Therefore, He mediates for us. He shares with God the person that we are and the person that we could become. He does this every day for those of us who have never spent a physical day face to face, or flesh to flesh with Him. Then there was Thomas, who touched Jesus' side, who confirmed by the shield of faith we believe. Jesus gives a report to God that only Christ can give because He looked into the depth of our hearts and saw beyond our foolishness that we cannot even present ourselves better, He sees that. Upon Him seeing that, He uses that information to give this report to God.

He does not have to advocate for us nor does He have to mediate for us, but He so chooses because He is thinks that is the best thing for us. It is who we are; that is the best there of. He looks for ways for us to be successful. Even if we do not turn out the way He pleases, He does. And finally, He is our intercessor. Having Christ within affords us gifts, specifically those that have believed in Me, believe that You have sent Me and have done the work that You sent Me to do. And I want to save them before I get to You, Father. I want to establish already this is who they are, I already want that established. As He intercedes on our behalf, He takes our concerns and who we are before His Father. It is with most assurance that I can say that He takes our needs seriously. He takes our desires seriously that He as looked at the inner thoughts of our heart and were able to give us seriously what it is we desire. He wants to give us these things because of what His experiences were while He was here. John, chapter 18 opens with 'when Jesus finished praying Jesus left with his disciples across the kindred valley on the other side there was an olive grove and He and His disciples went into it.' But in the Garden of Gethsemane, He prayed that He be excused but if He cannot be excused from this cup, may God's will be done. Shortly after that, it was.

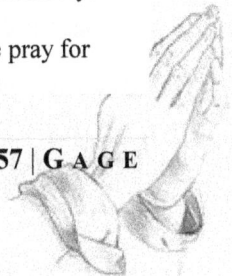

Understand that He is interceding for us all this time. In the depth of His intercession, the value of His intercession, and the purpose of His intercession keeps us whole. It keeps us focused on Him, and because we are focused on Him, we have to remember to focus on others as well. We are called to be intercessors for others. We are called to be advocates for others. We are called to be mediators for others because we are made in His image. So we want to remember that, we want to remember that intercession is a valuable gift. It is a gift. It is a gift that we need to really give more, more time to intercessory. We need to get to the point where we are beyond ourselves and that we pray for others fervently and diligently seeking out the needs of others and praying for them. That is what a real prayer warrior does. A prayer warrior puts down his or her things and prays on the spot, immediately so that the person who stands in the need of prayer leaves encouraged. The disciples witnessed His prayer life, His prayer times. His disciples saw what He is and what He was called to do. So the disciples knew that they needed to be available to do such things as well for others. And we should do the same.

What is God calling on us to do? Is He calling on us to be a prayer warrior? And if we are, why are we avoiding that job? Why are we avoiding the role? Why are we avoiding it? For what reason do we need to avoid it? We want to give to posture to what God needs for us to do as He is advocating, mediating and interceding for us. Likewise, we should do that for others. What does it take to give beyond ourselves? And do that for someone else? Whether we know them or not. Whether we know all the details or not. Can we go before the Father on the behalf of someone else? And do what Jesus has done for us? And that is the question. That is the outstanding poll. That is what is required. That is what we need. That is what we are here to do. That is what is supposed to be happening.

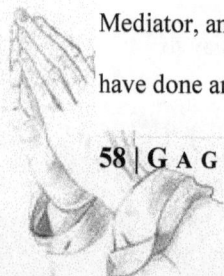

Father God, right now we thank You for being our Advocate, our Mediator, and our Intercessor. Jesus, we thank You right now for all that You have done and continue to do for us in our lives, and we apologize that we do not always understand that it is of You, Lord God, that these things always happen, we apologize for taking credit when we should not. And Lord God, we apologize for not sharing with others as we should. And so Lord, we are thankful that You are merciful and graceful unto us. All those things that we have, that we need, You supply. Thank You for Your protection. Thank You for Your encouragement. Thank You for Your teaching. And thank You for Your love. As we also ask God for forgiveness, in helping us as we forgive, diligently and fervently, others. We ask these blessings in Your Son Jesus' name. Amen.

As He Intercedes . . .

John 17:20-26 (NIV)

Jesus Prays for All Believers

[20] "My prayer is not for them alone. I pray also for those who will believe in me
through their message, [21] that all of them may be one, Father, just as you are in
me and I am in you. May they also be in us so that the world may believe that
you have sent me. [22] I have given them the glory that you gave me, that they may
be one as we are one— [23] I in them and you in me—so that they may be brought
to complete unity. Then the world will know that you sent me and have loved
them even as you have loved me.

[24] "Father, I want those you have given me to be with me where I am, and to see my glory, the glory you have given me because you loved me before the creation of the world.

[25] "Righteous Father, though the world does not know you, I know you, and they
know that you have sent me. [26] I have made you[a] known to them, and will
continue to make you known in order that the love you have for me may be in
them and that I myself may be in them."

Lord God, afresh we thank You Lord, as You prepare our hearts to receive this message. Lord our God, I thank You right now for giving us the courage of our convictions to pursue You with all that we have and all that we are, not all that we will become. Pursuing You in excellence, in spirit, and in truth without any thought or fashion regarding who is looking or who is paying attention or who knows. Lord God, I thank You right now what this word will impart to each of us. Thank You for using me as Your vessel, so Lord God I thank You right now that You completely take the reins. Do what it is You do. Lord God, allow me to follow Your lead. It is in Your Son Jesus' name I pray and ask these blessings. Lord, thank You for forgiving of me anything that might stand between You and me. It is in Your Son Jesus' name I pray. Amen.

AS HE INTERCEDES . . .

When you have an opportunity, I would like you to spend time reading the entire chapter of John 17. He spends the first five verses praying for Himself. He spends the next fourteen verses praying for others. Then He spends these last seven praying for the world and specifically as He prays for the world, He prays that they may be able to understand who Jesus Christ is and who God is. He makes some specific requests of His father that He might have an understanding of Him and of His glory and of His love and the abiding factor of a mutual relationship with all that said the purpose of prayer.

We talk about fair. Often people get caught up into what they need or what ails them or what they want that they forget why we are here. New people who are just getting into a relationship with prayer, not new to Christ necessarily, just a new relationship with prayer, often they do not have an understanding for what prayer is supposed to be. So when they have a situation where they enter in what I call the shallow end of the pool. This at means they have an inconsistent, 'all about me' prayer life. As Christians, we need to mature to a level where we can get more prayer time in, knowing when and how to pray for others, really talking to God with communion, where we are in an intimate dialogue.

This dialogue involves two people. I'm going to say some things, God is going to say some things, those things may or may not be in response to what I said, and what I said may or may not be in response to what God said. However, the intimacy developed in a time of prayer is awesome. As it is with any other relationship, you want to be able to foster that communication on a regular basis such that we are giving our time to God and God deserves it.

So as we jump right in here, he opens verse 20: "my prayer is not for them alone, I also pray for those who will believe in me through their message." He refers to believers, disciples if you will. He prays for them in the previous fourteen verses. He prays for them, the disciples, those who already believe in Jesus and those who follow Him, those who have had accepted Him as their Lord and Savior. So those who he refers to in text are those who will believe through the message of the disciples. My prayer is not for me. I pray for those persons who will believe in You through this message. Here is why that is important that he is praying. He is praying for us as disciples and that we disciple others.

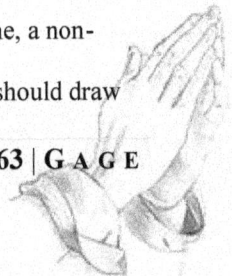

A disciple is called to disciple others. We have to use those words in the correct context, using the nouns and verbs correctly. At any time, a non-believer can be present. As a disciple, our words, deeds, activities should draw others to God, according to His will. Do understand that prayer is twofold: our part and God's part. A part of it is that they prayed with non-believers to get the message through those He sent and also prayer that we were going to be obedient to do the things we were sent to do. So the prayer is going to be very important that we understand how our calling, our gifts and the things that we are asked to do are done properly and in a timely fashion. When a non-believer is in a position where 'I can believe in Jesus Christ; He loves me,' the non-believer has benefitted from our prayers.

As we progress, Jesus is still talking to God. He uses the next couple of verses to discuss the unity He desires that all of us may be one with the Father just as you are in Me, and I am in you. This indwelling speaks of and is representative of John 15:5 where Jesus says 'I am The Vine. You are the branches. If you abide in Me and I will abide in you.' We want to be clear that relationship with Christ involves an indwelling. It requires an intimate relationship space. The I in Me and Me in Him gives you the effect of an intertwining. It is sort of like pretzels because you have to take the dough and twist it together and then loop it around and then it has that pretzel shape but that center is intertwined, the ends are pressed into the circle of the dough. This is the type of relationship He wants with us. This is not a regular relationship. He does not offer us something that is regular. It is definitely unique. It is definitely something that is hard to come by and harder to find and hardest to maintain.

We are designed to do this, designed to have this type of relationship. All we need to do is make it happen. Making it happen means that we invest more in God and in Christ and that way we can feel the investment that God and Christ have in us.

We have to invest in God. We do not invest in God like He invests in us. Prayer is the optimal place to make such a significant investment. Now understand the nature of His prayer is global. Jesus is a global intercessor. He prayed for Himself. He prays for the disciples. Then He prays for all believers and those who are yet to believe, those who are yet to answer the call. He has already placed in their life a desire to draw them nigh to Him, but they have not answered that call yet. He is not selfish in His prayer. We are not going to want God more than what God wants us, or want Christ more than Christ wants us. It is impossible. Though we have to figure out how to get to a prayer life that affords us the opportunity to abide in Him and He in us, there is really only us who stands in the way of that particular relationship.

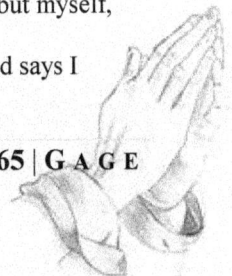

He is a global intercessor. He does not pray for just those who like Him, love Him, have accepted Him, and who follow Him. He does pray for people who are yet to accept Him as well. Again He is our example for things we should do. He as global intercessor deserves our attention. He prayed for those who despise Him as well. Now I will not speak for anybody but myself, however, I typically do not pray for my enemies as the word of God says I should. But He prays for all those who will believe and those who harmed Him. Meaning they have yet to believe regardless of who they are or how they got here or how they met, He is praying for all those who are yet to believe and those who do believe.

Because this is a global intercessory prayer, let us fast forward to Acts 9, we are on the road to Damascus. Jesus says to Paul, to Saul, "Who am I?" You see, without His prayer, many of us would not be Christians. This prayer extends into our lives over 2013 years later. It was clearly reality back then that the person who was most popular that benefited directly from that prayer, from those who were yet to believe through their message was Paul. See, Paul's preacher was Ananias. Paul's initial conversation was with Jesus. He sent Ananias to explain further and to close the deal. To give the benediction, if you will, understand that prayer is a function of what transformed in Paul. We have to ask ourselves when God prays for us at this level, with this level of intimacy, this level of full intimacy, what are we missing by not supplicating, not submitting to that prayer.

He is global. It is not about self. Very much about others and those who despise Him. Paul is an excellent example of how prayer changes us. The second thing the text teaches us is prayer which introduces God to all. We dealt with the global intercessor. We dealt with those who do not believe yet. We want to introduce God to all. Now, again, that is the nature of the church where we are today. Sharing Jesus Christ with others is called evangelism. By definition, I am not evangelistic in nature. I am a closet evangelist. If you get them here, I will close the deal. But you are a walking and talking evangelist. When you understand that God is represented by your walk as a Christian, then I cannot afford only to share Jesus at church or in other comfortable environments. We are responsible for sharing Jesus in spite of bad days, bad hair days, bad traffic days, bad husband days, bad wife days, bad kids days, bad car days, bad any days. Whatever your issue is, or your attitude is on any day or any occasion, God is the same God. He expects these same relationships. He expects the same behavior. He expects the same attitude. He expects the same representation. He expects the same modeling. He does not cut me any slack on my off days. He does not say, "Well Onedia is having a bad day today. I am going to excuse her from evangelizing today." The God that we serve will give me more opportunities to evangelize just to see if I will step out of my own funk and get past my own foolishness and selfishness and give of myself to another person during what I consider my weakness. He says for in our weakness that is when He is made strong. He shows the greatest amount of evidence when we feel we are nothing. That is when His evidence shines through.

So we have to give ourselves that type of credit. We have to give ourselves that type of activity. We have to give of ourselves in that fashion. We can say beyond a shadow of a doubt that we can pursue God through prayer with all that we are and all that we want to become and all that we are not and all that we were designed to be all at the same time and know that and be secure in that.

God is going to do exactly what He said He would. Now, verse 25, this prayer to which he refers, [25] "Righteous Father, though the world does not know You, I know You, and they know that You have sent Me." The Great I Am, because He sent Me. The disciples try to get Him off task. He says, "Saving souls is why I have been sent." When His mother tried to get Him off task, He said, "This is not why I have been sent." He honors her request because He has to honor His mother, but He told her this is not my time; this is not My season. So we need to understand as a prayer warrior, Jesus is global. As we expand our prayer boundaries of who we pray for, we need to be led to ask God for a discerning spirit for when to say would you like me to pray for you, what is on your prayer lists, what are your prayer concerns, and be trusted with that information. Do we ask people to intercede on their behalf?

The Lord aligns people and when He aligns people together, because of the power of intercession and because of the power of each individual's testimony, the person you intercede on the behalf of may also be the person who needs the testimony, which is when the transparency is required. We need to get past ourselves and start praying for other people. At this point, it does not matter if you know them or not. I know a lot of people because I facilitate classes. They are my students. They will not share their prayer requests, but they will bring the requests on behalf of someone else and they do some of that is because they do not think that they have what they consider major concerns. They do not give those concerns away in public. They do not feel the need for two or more to be joined together. Now the unfortunate part of that is God is taken out of the equation. It is not ok for you determine whether or not God needs to bless you before others. You need to be willing to give Him everything. I have heard a preacher recently say that you do not need to ask God to go to Whataburger, if you are hungry just go. On the other hand, I heard another preacher say you should pray over every single thing, 'Lord what would you have me eat?' Let me tell you why that person wants to ask God what would You have me to eat. She has the gift of evangelism. She wants to know based on the decision that she makes how likely is it she would have an opportunity to share Jesus Christ during that event, so the prayer is Lord where would You have me to eat such that I may give You the most glory and honor.

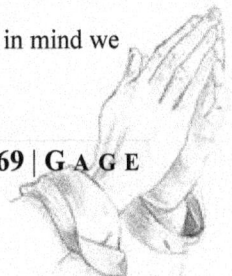

So ask yourselves when we make these commitments or these professions, or we have these conversations, what exactly are we saying? What exactly are we praying about? Why are we here? It becomes very important that we get into a place where we understand ourselves well enough to be able to go into the spirit of intercession as Christ has modeled for us, pray globally for people to believe in God, and know that Jesus was sent to save their souls. He died, was buried and resurrected as the savior of our sins. So, keep in mind we said Jesus is a global intercessor. We cannot offer prejudice against people who we do not know, or we think we hate because of some things they have done. We have to be global intercessors so that all may come to Christ but through the message I deliver, through the message that you deliver. Sometimes it is not the message you deliver, rather it is your walk. It is your attitude. It is your demeanor. It is your compassion. It is your ability to help. It is your ability to serve. It is all these things. It is all these things. So as we prepare for those who do not believe yet, sometimes you are just going to be a planter. You are going to plant these seeds and introduce Christ. 'You know Onedia, I do not ever remember you mentioning that you go to church. Do you have a church home? Are you in a relationship with Christ? Based on the answers, you are going to invite them to church. Likewise, you can ask, 'Well do you mind if I share with you my Lord and Savior? Do you mind if I share with you who it is?' Great let's get started.

Some Christians have just lost their way. Something happened, the death of a loved one, you were promised you would heal, He did not promise healing on this side, He just promised healing: all causing you to abandon prayer, and abandon God. Now they are healed, and they are on the other side. So we need to get to that point where we are able to pray for those for who do not believe yet and willing, when the opportunity opens itself up, to share Christ and God with that person. So we have to pray globally. I want to pray and seek out specifically nonbelievers and introduce them to Christ. Now, as we introduce God to all, we are going to run into some opposition. What we cannot do is let that opposition discourage us or sway us in a different direction. So we pray that we may be strengthened in our walk, in our words. We do not want anything to befall us, from this situation. I was talking to someone about the fact that I missed some opportunities to evangelize, I missed some opportunities to share Christ, but now when I meet people who say you look familiar I say, 'Well where do you go to church?' They give me the practice that I need to talk to strangers about Christ. This gives me the opportunity to share Jesus.

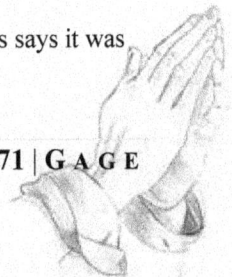

So also when we introduce God to all, we want to remember why we are doing it. You did not bring anyone to Christ; you participated in the process. You see last year someone said I want to invite you to church with me. Six months later someone said I want to invite you to bible study with me. Two months later our church is having a women's conference at church. Would you like to come? And by the time they got to you or ran across your path, you have become bold enough to ask. You had the training to carry the mission out. You can help them make a decision and point them in the right direction. You did not do anything. All of that activity was orchestrated by God. All of that was put together by God. So we want to be careful that the right person gets the glory. It is like your career when you give your presentation to your boss, and your boss takes your presentation to the meeting and in the meeting your boss says it was his presentation. He gets thanked, and he never says it was you who did the work. It is the same thing when you take credit for someone else's work. That is called plagiarism, and we are not trying to plagiarize the glory of God. It belongs to Him. We did not do it. So God encourages us to pray, Jesus models prayer for us and shares with us a gift in a dynamic fashion what was given of Him. Jesus shows us the prayer essentials. We cannot live without it, and it is so powerful to help others come to Christ.

Lord God, I thank You for this time and this word. I thank You for this message as You unfold it before us Lord God. I thank You that You were able to do exceedingly and abundantly more than we could ever ask or think. Lord God, now I thank You for using me. Thank You for creating in me a clean heart, Lord God. I thank You right now for Your service, and I thank You for the fervency and my sense of urgency. Lord God, thank You for the work ethic as I am in pursuit of You. Lord God, I thank You right now for the person's whose lives will be changed, enhanced, enriched, and encouraged by the words that we have heard today. Lord God, I thank You again for your love and kindness, in Your Son's Jesus' name we pray. Amen.

The Prejudice of Prayer

Matthew 26:36-39 (NIV)

Gethsemane

36 Then Jesus went with his disciples to a place called Gethsemane, and he said
to them, "Sit here while I go over there and pray." 37 He took Peter and the two
sons of Zebedee along with him, and he began to be sorrowful and
troubled. 38 Then he said to them, "My soul is overwhelmed with sorrow to the
point of death. Stay here and keep watch with me."

39 Going a little farther, he fell with his face to the ground and prayed, "My
Father, if it is possible, may this cup be taken from me. Yet not as I will, but as
you will."

Father God, we thank You for this day, for this vessel, for this time, for this hour to talk about prayer and the prejudice of prayer. We thank You, Lord God right now that You are going to give us exactly what we need today. Lord, remove anything that hinders me from serving You with the fullness of what it is that You have called on me to do. Lord God, I thank You right now for the ministry You have gifted me with and what You give me to do, so Lord God I thank You right now for Your Son Jesus, for forgiveness of my sins. It is in your Son Jesus' name that I pray and ask these blessings. Amen.

THE PREJUDICE OF PRAYER

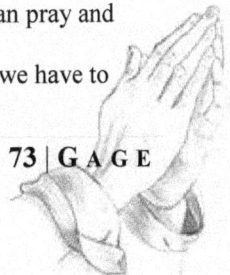

The Prejudice of Prayer. This is a famous place called Gethsemane and in the Gethsemane Garden, it is that place where Jesus feels He can pray and take refuge to the Lord; and so because He has made this choice, we have to honor it as well. What do we mean by honor it? Well, first of all, let us set up our scene; let us talk about where we are here. Let us talk about what is supposed to be happening. Let us be clear that Jesus has always been mobile. He was always walking. He was always moving around, but Jesus is very in tune with the Lord; He is very in tune with His Father. He does not avoid conversations. He does not avoid the interactions that He and the Lord are designed to have. So, it is no surprise that He seeks God during this situation, in this season. There is the prejudice of this prayer. In verse 26, He announces His time of prayer. When He announces His time of prayer, that announcement should have done several things to the disciples.

His announcement should have gotten their attention to the point of shock and awe. There should be some shock and awe value when Jesus said, "I'm going to pray." You see the Lord our God, Jesus Christ has the answers. He knows what is coming, He knows what is forthcoming. He knows what to anticipate. So, when He says, "I'm going off to pray," the disciples should have been able to discern from that – gather from that – assume even, that this is a serious time. Now, that announcement followed the fact that Jesus predicted Peter's denial. Peter was on this trip when He said, "Stay here while I go over there and pray." The statement opens up my sanctified imagination. I'm asking myself, "What are the disciples thinking? What could they possibly be pondering at this moment?" The scripture paints a picture in verse 37 that 'He began to be sorrowful and troubled, and He announced He was going off to pray.' I cannot find or recall any time where He says, "I'm going off to pray." He just starts praying. He prayed when they were not around. He prayed when He sent them over in a boat. He prays but He never announces it prior to this point but now He announces, "I'm going to pray." I would have to ask myself some questions as a disciple: What does God want me to do? Should I be praying with Jesus? Should I be asking questions like, "Lord, do You want me to pray with You? Is there something we are praying for specifically? Lord, may I hear?" This makes me so curious that out of Peter's normal character, he did not say, "Let me hear – let me hear." I want to know what You tell God when You leave us to pray; I would have to ask to let me hear.

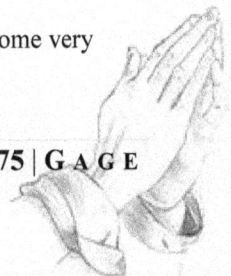

With prayer being as intimate as it is and having as much power as it does, it seems like a follower of Christ I would want to get in there and find out what is being said. Jesus is very serious; He becomes troubled, He becomes sorrowful. Again, using my sanctified imagination and my forethought or my intuition, I am wondering as well does the point where Jesus says, "I'm going to pray," should I be considering what is going to happen next? He is troubled and sorrowful. Like Jesus, I am wondering, "Did I get everything done? Am I leaving anything out?" I know there is going to become a time that I am going have to go through these things that I have already been told about. Is there anything I am leaving out of this? The prejudice of prayer has become very personal, the prejudice of prayer is also very private, and the very prejudice of prayer is it is very productive.

Verse 38 answers my preliminary questions; it reads: "Then he said to them, my soul is overwhelmed with sorrow to the point of death; stay here and keep watch with me." He answers several of those questions right there, "I'm overwhelmed; My earthly time is coming to an end." He is aware of that. Shortly after these verses, there is going to come a time, about ten verses from here, that He's going to be arrested; the arrest process starts; the accuser, His betrayer comes forward. And still no conversation from the disciples. No attention from the disciples. No attentiveness from the disciples. There is nothing that says the disciples understand all that they have done thus far. Every one of these days they have spent walking with Him for these three years – nothing tops this moment. Nothing tops this occasion because whatever happens next is really the end of our intimate training face to face. At the beginning of the world, this moment was planned. We have to ask ourselves, "Is that something we are ready to do." We have to ask ourselves, "Are we indeed equipped to serve at that level where He says 'stay here and keep watch with Me'?" In our private, personal, productive prayer time with the prejudice of prayer, we have to ask ourselves, 'If people are coming around us that we run into on a daily basis are we doing this to them?' If they say, "Pray with me, keep watch with me," then are we being the person that we are called to be? Are we doing what it is we are called to do? Inside of that we have to ask ourselves, “Are we being private, personal and productive in our prayers?”

There is a certain amount of allegiance we have to pay to these scriptures and treat them with care. Inside these scriptures, Jesus has wrapped us up in the compassion that we should have for other people. It seems as if it is very hard for the disciples to really understand when they need to step up and do the disciple job. So, with that being said – verse 39, ‘going a little farther, He fell with His face to the ground and prayed, “My Father, if it is possible, let this cup pass from Me; yet not as I will, but as You will.”’

Let us talk about the productivity of the prejudice of prayer. “Going a little farther” may have been out of their range of hearing, maybe even out of their range of vision. What He does with this going farther piece is seeking somewhere that is private. He takes a very personal stance for Himself. He is very productive in getting to the point: going a little farther, He fell with His face to the ground. We talk about being prostrate before the Lord, being out in front of God. We talk about that, but do we really give reverence to God in our most humble state, in our most humble state we are prostrate in front of God. We are not postured. We have not positioned ourselves in a posture that gets His attention. We need to position ourselves in a posture that gets His complete and undivided attention because we do not have anything. We are not standing there arrogantly. We are not kneeling on just one knee. We are on the ground, face down completely surrendered to God.

This prayer posture produces again, productivity—it produces the greatest amount of results. If we want to position ourselves to understand that this prayer is just an intensive prayer – this is an intentional, “God, I need to share with You who I am and I need to give You all of me right now at this hour, no turning back – it is because it is Your will that I am trying to get accomplished. It is because of You that I exist, and it is because of where we are in this life that I am here at this moment in time. Based on those things, I come before You Lord in the most humble position I know. Jesus being our example and teacher of prayer, models exactly what it is we have been asked for all this time, to give ourselves in the most proficient, authentic fashion and here we are.

“My Father, if it is possible, may this cup be taken away from Me?” He gives Him honor and respect as “My Father” and He asks Him to reconsider His position, reconsider His promise He made, reconsider the words He has already published years and years before, preached by prophets long before His birth, conception, knowledge of, before the first miracle – years before - “if it is possible.” And this cup is a metaphor for the road ahead: His purpose, His calling. The metaphor He is about to embark upon is His death, burial and resurrection. At the point of the arrest, it becomes a formality; it becomes a check the box: this is going to happen, I know that this is where we are headed.

But not getting outside of that we want to stay right here and say, "May this cup be taken away from Me." It is a sentence. It is not technically a question; by virtue of your punctuation it is a sentence, it is a statement. In view of the request, it is not a question. Now, I want to tell you right there between me and you, there is a period, there is a space. In parentheses, I want to add right there, and I did not argue with my God, my Father: I do not beg. I do not plea. I do not reason. I do not negotiate. I simply said, "Yet not as I will but as You will," again, with a very open spirit under the very prejudice of prayer.

We take the prejudice of prayer too far. We want it our way, right now, how we see fit, because it is what we desire for our own selves, without any knowledge of what God's will is or how this impacts the rest of our lives or what this means to everybody before us and after us. Jesus had no problem with saying this is really about to happen, "I am going to make a plea and I hope that My plea is understood. If it is not understood then I am going to do what it is I can to make that happen. Not My will but Thy will be done."

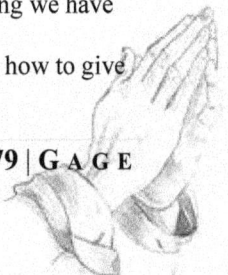

When we say thy will be done, we have to be able to completely submit to God, and we have to understand what that means. It cannot be a by-product nor can it be a half-hearted request. It has to be a totally dedicated and committed request and if it is a totally committed request, submission is required. We have to be clear about that and that clarity is something we have to be focused on for the prejudice of prayer. You cannot figure out how to give that clarity without understanding who is in charge. You see, we try to split the "in chargeness" with God, then we want to negotiate: well, I will take these responsibilities, You take these over here. That is not how it works, that is not how it works at all: we have got to ask ourselves, "How do I submit to God and completely submit to Him without this additive of 'well I am going to negotiate with You and then I am going to negotiate and negotiate and negotiate with You until I persuade You to give me my way.'" God does not negotiate.

There is a point when we really surrender and truly give ourselves over in a fashion that God can be proud of, in a fashion that we can discern as to what God has for us and His will. Jesus knew when He got here what His role was. He told it to the disciples; He let them know this is what I am here for. "It is by design that I'm here– okay?" Because He told us what we were designed for, we should get in that role and stay there. We have such a hard time following those directions and being able to give of ourselves and give to Him the us He desires. We misunderstand that the prejudice of prayer does come with some specific limitations.

You see, we have learned how to pray in Matthew 6: "thine will be done on earth as it is in heaven – thine will be done." At all times "thine will be done" because it is what You design for me. This prayer could have gone a little differently; this prayer could have been seen differently, edited different, shaped differently, fulfilled differently, and spent differently. This time could have looked differently, but let us get back to all the characters: let us talk about the disciples for just a moment.

At a time when it is truly critical to pay attention to your Master, the disciples are not really engaged. We learn later exactly what they are doing, but they are not really engaged – they are not really engaged. With our knowledge of the prejudice of prayer, how can we engage better in what we are called to do? How can we be engaged better in what God wants from us? How can we be engaged better what the designs of our lives are? That is the part of the prejudice of prayer we need to consider; we need to get engaged at a higher level. At that higher level, we want to elevate our prayer life to such a level so when I go before the Father, I truly submit to His will, I truly submit to His way and I truly give to Him the glory, honor and praise because He is worthy. I want Him to recognize that while I am under the prejudice of prayer where it is perfectly permissible to go forward and request all the things I desire, knowing that I should go back and submit completely to His will. Some of His will erases what it is that I desire – it may not erase my desire but it does erase the fact that this is never going to happen. So we have to ask ourselves, "How do we get to the point where we say to ourselves that I am going to submit to Your will? I am going to give you what you deserve. I am going to be Your child and ask You to allow this one to pass me but if it does not – if it should not pass me, thank You for the ability to withstand the storm or the consequence or all of those things so that we can understand: Thine will be done – Thine will be done."

That prejudice of prayer is permissive to God because it is private in nature, that it is personal in its character and that it is productive for God's will to be done. Prayer is going to produce within our activity and behavior what He needs from us to go on and do His will further. Jesus never quits. He never stops doing what He was doing. He never stops functioning. He did not just shut down because it did not go His way. He did not tell the disciples, "Head on down the road because I need some time by Myself because I am about to do some things you all do not understand." While that was true, He did not respond to them in that fashion – He did not respond to them in that manner at all, yet He was able to be Jesus in a fashion that He could give us of Himself without concern, without being consumed with the wrong thing.

The Prejudice of Prayer.

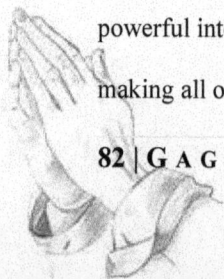

Father God, how we bless You and love You and pray this day for this message, this word. Thank You for this vessel. Thank You for what we will go forward and do on behalf of You, Lord God, and in Your will. Father, allow us to stay inside of the will You created for us, Lord God. Thank You for giving us Yourself. Thank You for giving us Your Son. Thank You for giving us the most powerful intercessor, the Holy Spirit. We thank You right now that You are making all of us disciples so that we can go ye therefore and understand the value of being laid out prostrate before You with the prejudice of prayer on our heart because it is private, personal and productive. And Lord God, we thank You that it is permissible. Lord, we just thank You right now for the humbleness that You will instill and impart upon each of us and allow us to bless You through others. So Lord God, we thank You now afresh for doing what only You can do in Your Son Jesus' name we pray this prayer.

Amen.

The Discipline of Prayer

Matthew 26:40-41 (NIV)

[40] Then he returned to his disciples and found them sleeping. "Couldn't you men
keep watch with me for one hour?" he asked Peter. [41] "Watch and pray so that
you will not fall into temptation. The spirit is willing, but the flesh is weak."

Lord God, afresh we thank You this day, for Your power, Your presence and the might of the Holy Spirit. Lord, we thank You right now for the discipline of prayer. We thank You for Your provision of prayer. We thank You for all that You provide for us. Lord, we thank You for the forgiveness of our sins. We thank You right now for providing us our daily bread. And Lord God, we thank You right now for just doing what only You can do and we appreciate You for that. And Lord God, I thank You for this vessel that You may use me today in a mighty way that whoever might hear this word will go away empowered, enriched, encouraged and will seek You for their needs for those things that deeply concern them. In Your Son Jesus' name, I pray and ask His blessings.

Amen.

THE DISCIPLINE OF PRAYER

In our scriptures today, Jesus is in the Garden of Gethsemane and in the previous four verses He is overwhelmed to the point of death because He knows that His hour is coming and He is going to have to face His accusers. He is about to face the part of being able to be tried, that He is going to die, be buried and be resurrected. Because of that, He is very disturbed. He takes this time to go pray because He is deeply concerned and He wants to share with the Lord how He is concerned – He wants to share with God what concerns Him. And so with this, these two verses, we have transitioned into Him sharing with the disciples. He has asked the disciples to keep watch; just sit there and keep watch. I want you to just spend some time with it knowing that Jesus is telling them what needs to happen. Anyway, that brings us to our current scene where He returns from prayer and He returns to them and they are sleeping.

Now, the discipline of prayer is where we are today. The discipline of prayer requires several things: **1.** It requires our attention, our focus; **2.** It requires us to understand our calling for our aptitude; and **finally**, it requires our ability to be alert – so between those three things is the discipline of prayer. **Our attention. Our aptitude. Our alertness.**

One of the things that we should know about being a disciple is that God is attentive and detailed. There is a certain amount of attention that God pays to the smallest of details which requires our attention, we should be focused on those same types of details. In the previous verses again, you would have to spend time reading to get the back story and understand deeply that God has prepared them for what is to come. When God prepares us for those things, we have to be paying attention. Jesus tells them, "Keep watch while I go pray." Jesus puts them on alert. He gives them the notice that something is going on and explains to them by saying, "I'm sorrowful." He just previously predicted His death. He has just predicted Peter's denial. He just served the Lord's Supper, so the intimate time He is spending with His disciples is of importance; our walk with Jesus requires a certain level of attention. We have to stay focused and remember, "I need to pay attention. God is calling upon me to do something and I have to pay attention or I have to be able to say this is what I have been called to do." Whatever it is that God is calling upon you to do, you have to say to yourself: "Self, this is what I'm being asked of me." So understand that in this period of time we cannot take our eye off the ball and that is what happens to us when we get distracted. Excuses are unacceptable. We have no reason why we should take our eye off the ball and think that it is ok. No way we should get unfocused and sidetracked behind what it is that we are supposed to be doing. There is no time for that. There is no way we should do that and so because we get off focus because of various reasons, we need to be reminded of the importance of that focus.

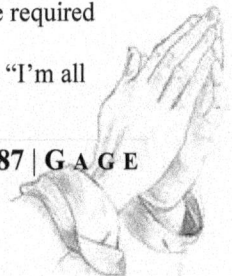

Now we need to get back in line with the word of God, our intimacy with God, being able to focus on God, and that focus is going to be required because we have an assignment from God. So when we talk about "I'm all focused," what is it that we mean? You see, we do not have the privilege to reach out and touch Jesus by the hand nor say that, "Jesus, we are touching You by the hand because You are right here in our presence." We need the help of one another in the Holy Spirit and being able to be in tune and mature enough with the word to know that when God says "keep watch" in these scriptures it applies to us as well. We have to say to ourselves, "What does it take for me to keep watch?" When I say "keep watch," what does it mean to keep watch today? Back in Gethsemane, He wanted them to sit down and pray, so to keep watch today means that we need to stay focused and be prayerful too. We need to watch for the enemy's schemes. We need to watch for people who we assigned to serve. We as a people, as a Christian faith, as a Christian group, we spend way too much time giving the enemy credit. We need to spend more time giving Jesus credit, as well as the Holy Spirit, and God, the authority and glory. "The devil made me do it." I'm tired of hearing that because that is number 1, not true, but number 2, and most importantly, you have an escape route and did you seek the escape route? The answer is no; but we have to say to ourselves, "Self, what do I need to do? Self, what needs to take place?" So that we can go on and do what He says. So keep watch means that we are going to:

1. **We are going to stay focused and pray,**
2. **We are going to study His word,**
3. **We are going to apply and do what It says,**

4. **We are going to share – we are going to share that word, share our Christian spirit, evangelize if you will, get others and show them who God is and why He is who He is.**

We want to take care of God's business because He takes care of our business. and keeping watch means that we are attentive to what He requires of us – we are attentive to what it is He requires of us.

Now, our next point is that **we have an aptitude**. Aptitude is known as knowledge. There is a cliché: "your aptitude does not determine your altitude but your attitude determines your altitude." To a large extent I can see that, but our aptitude about Christ is going to determine what we need to do next - what do we need to do next? What we need to do next is understand what God has for us – what does He have for us to do? In this scenario, He says, "sit here and keep watch." Did Jesus need a guard at the gate? No. When we talk about the aptitude, the decision to keep watch with Him for an hour should be an instant decision. Knowing God and being able to understand His ways is what we were focused on at that time. We should have been working on the information about God we had before. We missed an opportunity. We did not put our knowledge of Christ to work and sometimes that is what our problem is – we do not put our knowledge of Christ to work. Because we did not put our knowledge of Christ to work, then we fell short of pleasing and serving God the way He desired and requested. Maybe we do not put our knowledge to work because we not have enough knowledge.

He allowed His disciples to walk with Him for about three years and at the close of these three years is going to be His death, burial and resurrection but you walked around with Christ. Keeping watch should not have been this tough at whatever time of day or night this is. He asked them specifically, "You could not keep watch for an hour? You could not stay awake till I got back?"

That is how it is today, "You cannot keep from being distracted till I get back?" We have the benefit of the entire Bible. It is bound in leather and many other fabrics. "Now it is electronically available and you mean to tell me that you cannot keep watch until I return? You have got the benefit of the whole word in written form and you mean to tell me you cannot keep watch over My business for this short period of time? I have only asked you to keep watch over My business." I want to be clear that we have asked ourselves what to do. We have to ask ourselves what we are supposed to be doing. We cannot keep claiming it is someone else's fault. We have to ask ourselves what are we supposed to be keeping watch over and with the knowledge we have of Christ, how do we simply move forward with that knowledge – equipped by Christ to move forward so that we are able to do what it is that He's called us to do.

We have a certain level of aptitude and that aptitude is going to give us what we need to serve Him so we can keep watch and while this scripture text for us is a proverbial hour, but for Him it really was an hour. And what if we kept watch hour by hour, what could we accomplish? What if we can measure the hour at which we precisely took our eye off of what God wants us to do? If we took our eye off of what God wants us to do at that particular hour, say it was 6 o'clock, then we will know how to correct ourselves tomorrow when it is time to keep watch at 6 o'clock: "do not go left, go right" and that way, we can get ourselves in a situation where we need to move forward and we need to take care of what it is we are called to do. That gives us the latitude we need to make our efforts worthwhile everyday because that is what we need. It is the aptitude to make proper decisions every day, every hour until He returns, given that we understand our calling, given that we have been paying attention with the amount of detail that is required to follow Christ. This is not something that you can do without a level of detail. This is not something that you can do without a sense of urgency. This is something you have to do with both of those and then some. This is something you have to do with that very activity in mind. You cannot (and I repeat) you cannot afford to avoid, you have to stay focused on what it is that God requires of each of us and that focus requires your attention and our attitude.

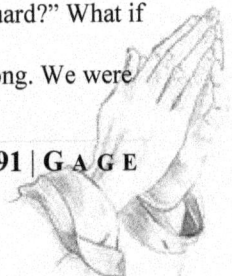

Lastly, we want to cover **our alertness**. I alluded to it earlier but our alertness is going to give you the problem that most of us have, or the lack thereof. We like eye candy. We like things that are pretty. We like things that have color to them. We crave those types of things. Those things give us joy; we look at them and get excited. When our alertness is required, we have to remain alert to keep watch. What if "keep watch" means "stand guard?" What if it means be a bodyguard for Jesus? He was not doing anything wrong. We were not peeping. We were not the lookout but what if we were needed to stand guard against His aggressors? Alertness is required – remember that adage about the wolf in sheep's clothing. You want to be aware to of people who say: "You know I believe in Jesus" but they mean "hesus." I know you all are laughing when I say that but you have to be careful because what you believe in everybody does not believe in. What you are keeping watch over? Everybody is not keeping watch over the same things. What is important to you is not important to other people, so then you find yourself trying to figure out what exactly you are supposed to be doing. Inside of that, you find yourself not paying attention, not exercising your own aptitude, and you are distracted, the definition of unalert.

I recently watched a movie entitled "The Call." My daughter thinks the movie is very cool and she really likes it; however, it is a rated R movie. The opening of the movie starts with a teenaged girl, high school student walking in the mall parking lot looking down at her cell phone. Now for those of you who are parents, and particularly those of you who are men, you are already upset because the first thing you tell us about walking in the mall parking lot is to stay alert, stay on focus and do not be on your cell phone while you are walking. That is the first thing you say – you say that to your wife, your girlfriend, your best friend. You say that to your aunt, your mother, your cousins – you say that to all these people in your life, but what do they do? They walk in the parking lot on their cell phone and you have said this a million times.

We are not alert for what Christ has asked us to do, we are not alert. We are not staying alert to what it is we are called to do. God has to call our name several different times to get our attention several different ways in order to spark in us a response after He's called on us to do something in His will because we are looking around at the wrong thing—distracted.

I like it when the Holy Spirit taps me on my shoulder and say: "I said, do such and such – I said, do blah blah." What that means is that I am looking at the Lord and I am saying to Him, "I am paying attention to You. I am doing what You say to do. I am in line with what You have asked of me." That is not to say that that makes me any better than anybody else but what it says is that I am paying attention to what it is that God is wanting of me, my surroundings. You see, I do not want to get captured by satan, I do not want him to know what I am doing. I do not want him to be able to tell me he can see me do what I do. I do not want him to have a detail of what I have going on. I want to listen to God and at that particular point in time be able to respond in kind. My alertness is required to do a good job that He already planned in advance for me to do – my alertness is required! Specifically in verse 41, Jesus says: "So you do not fall into temptation – so you do not fall into the hands of the enemy. By any means, that is very important to our walk. So it is your attention, your aptitude and your alertness that is required by God for the discipline of prayer.

So Father God, we thank You right now for the discipline of prayer and all those things that You are requiring of us. Lord, we thank You for the ability to remain attentive, to remember our aptitude, our knowledge and to remember to be alert at all times for what it is You have for us. For what it is signals, You are sending to us to stay on path.

Lord God, we thank You right now for Jesus who hung, bled and died and was resurrected for our sins.

Lord God, we thank You right now for forgiving us of those sins daily and thanking You for forgetting those things that we have done that are so wrong to You, Lord God.

We thank You right now for those whose lives we have touched, whose lives we understand better, and whose lives we will just become part of because of the love you have for us.

I ask this in Your Son Jesus' name we pray.

Amen.

The Sacrifice of Prayer

Matthew 26:42-46 (NIV)

42 He went away a second time and prayed, "My Father, if it is not possible for this cup to be taken away unless I drink it, may your will be done."

43 When he came back, he again found them sleeping, because their eyes were
heavy. 44 So he left them and went away once more and prayed the third time,
saying the same thing.

45 Then he returned to the disciples and said to them, "Are you still sleeping and
resting? Look, the hour has come, and the Son of Man is delivered into the
hands of sinners. 46 Rise! Let us go! Here comes my betrayer!"

Lord God, how we bless You and thank You on this day.

There are times when we have put You in the hands of the betrayer by our behavior and our activities, our attitude and our disposition. Lord, we thank You right now that You are going to give us what we need today to overcome those things that so easily entangle us.

Hear us Lord God! We thank You afresh because You are God and God alone. Because of that God-sized love and of that God-sized being O God, we thank You right now just for giving us the opportunity or chance to do what it is You have for us to do.

Thank You for Your vessel this day Lord God, that You can give to me what it is that You have for me to do. Thank You for giving me an assignment. Thank You for thinking that I am trustworthy enough to carry it out.

Lord God, I thank You today for why we are here and what we will learn, what we will hear and how we will grow.

In Your Son, Jesus' name we pray and ask His blessings.

Amen.

The Sacrifice of Prayer

Every day it is recommended, suggested, advised that we spend time with God. We talk about 10% of everything belongs to God that includes 10% of your time, but you know I have had to debate the point. It seems silly that I would have to argue with someone that you owe 10% of your time every day to God. Those who are wise give God some of the time back that He gives them. He gives you 24 whole hours to do basically what you please. He asks that we serve Him, worship Him, praise and give Him honor and glory. Inside of that 24 hours we need to find 2 hours and 24 minutes that we may dedicate and give over to Him. And do so willingly. Understanding that 2 hours and 24 minutes seems like a whole lot. People ask me how did you find that out and I respond, "Oh you know, you just do the math – 24 hours and 10% of 24 hours is 2.4 hours. 4/10 x 24/60 gives us 2 hours and 24 minutes." People are very stunned and taken aback, and I say, "How much time of yours belongs to God? Did you give yourself that time? Why wouldn't you want to give your Creator some of your time? If you do not give Him some time, what kind of relationship are you in with God?" As I mentioned I have debated this from time to time with Christians and they would look strange and say, "How did you come up with that number?" They ask as if I made it up myself. It is biblical! It is in Malachi 3:10. It talks about 10% as the tithe. It says everything you have belongs to God - everything: your face, your hair, your time, your financial resources, your talents, your gifts because you did not create any of that yourself. A self-made man is the most foolish one of them all: "I made myself, I did this by myself." Really? Let us see if you really can do it by yourself: breathe, think, feel, walk, talk – let Him cut it off, let Him cut off His power, His anointing, and let us see what you really can do by yourself.

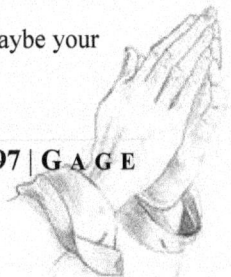

When is your time with God? We need to figure out some time to spend with God. We need to give God some authentic and genuine time. Not that time on the run when we are on our way to somewhere. Not just our time in church because it is as though it is something you learned to do. It is something to do right before you go to brunch – not that kind of time. Some time when no one is looking. You do not have on your Sunday's best. You do not have on your chicest clothes. Maybe you are wearing your pajamas. Maybe you are wearing your robe, or your loungewear and your house slippers. Maybe your hair is still wrapped in a bun. You look shaken from the night's sleep, but you give your first fruits to God because your first mind goes straight to God. I am talking about some quiet time in the morning immediately when you wake up.

First. Before you check your phone, before you update your status on Facebook even if it is a scripture - the time you give to God should be first. Let us look at that type of time. And again, because we are so busy with a lower case "b," we want to ensure that we are giving of ourselves in an authentic manner, which demonstrates we care about those things that God cares about. We care about those things that God says concerns God, and that is prayer. Now I understand there might be a sacrifice of your but I think that is a God who gives you those reasons why you could be busy or God could take all of that away so He can get your full undivided attention at any time is worth whatever sacrifice you made. I want us to always consider that. God can take away that job and those accoutrements – that car, that house, that husband, that wife, and that job. He can take all those things taken away and get your attention: ask Job. He can have all of those taken away, and He would have your full, undivided attention. I bet you then you could find some time, the time to commune with God.

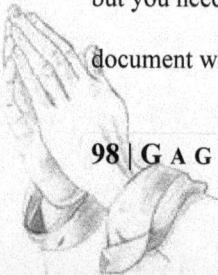

Present what your truth is just as you believe it. We started at verse 42, but you need to know that there are several scriptures ahead of this which document what has happened in this encounter with Christ. The disciples had been brought to the Garden of Gethsemane and Jesus is going to go pray. He had gotten to the point where He is sorrowful to death. He knows that His time has come. Everything He has prepared up until this point is all because of what is about to happen next. At the beginning of these scriptures, He is going to pray for a second time. He says, "Father I want this cup taken away, but if not, I will humbly submit to Your will. I will give You what it is You said that You wanted Me to do." That is a bold statement for Christ, He knows, but He is asking one more time, "Lord God, is there anything that we can do differently such that I do not have to die." Present what your truth is just as you believe it. Oftentimes, when I talk to people about prayer, they have a posture where they present prayer in such a fashion that if they told it to you, you would say no as well. So imagine what they are saying to a God, who is all knowing, all present and your Creator, and obviously He knows even more about you than you know about yourself. Let us understand that you present this truth in a wavering manner – that is not the God we serve. If you do not believe yourself, what you are saying, those words which come out of your mouth, the fact that God can do exceedingly abundantly above all we can ever ask and/or think, then you do not deserve it. When you present what your truth is as you believe it, and you present it in a lack luster, mediocre manner, you should not get what you have asked for. In Revelation, He says that if you are lukewarm I want to spit you out of My mouth. So if you come to Him half-heartedly, sort of kind of not quite believing what it is that you present then you should not get what you have asked for: you should not get it. That is just my opinion, you should not get it.

I have children and when they come to me and say: "Mommy, may I have X Y and Z?" I ask them immediately, "Why? Why should I give you that?" And if you cannot sustain your argument well enough, then the answer is "no." If you want something: a toy or a trinket or even some clothes because someone else has it, the answer is "no." If you want it because it is something you really like and you really want it, you are going to take care of it, and you are ready for the responsibility associated with your request, then I am on my way to the cash register with this request. But I did not buy it just because you asked for it, I bought it because of the thought that you have placed into this, and you believe in what you asked for. Likewise, I believe that God only answers me - if we do not have a certain amount of production behind our request, then we are not going to get it. If you ask Him for something and not believing that He can or/and will, then we should not have it, we should not have it. That is a perfunctory request, and we should not ask Him for that. He should not offer it to us either; we do not deserve it. But if we are going to ask something of Him, ask with vigor and fervor and zeal and passion and compassion. Ask Him with a sense of urgency, with a warm and engaged spirit for He is wise enough to see your heart in that scenario and determine that this is really something that is important.

Present what your truth is as you believe it. This also means we are not going to come up with some malarkey – yes, I used that word – malarkey to Jesus, to Christ, to God, to the Holy Spirit. The caveat with that is as you believe it. Do not start making up things. You have to know that God is going to help us move towards His will, and His will is going to be found within us at the appropriate time. So we can come to Him with the right information, at the right time, doing the right thing, because asking for things that we have made up or asking for things in a disingenuous manner is not going to get us where we aim to go, so I want us to make sure that "as you believe" is not something that we have conjured up and present something that is foolish to God.

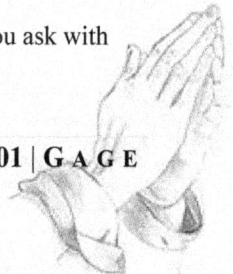

Then there is prostrate before God. In an earlier verse, it says, "going a little farther He fell with His face to the ground and prayed" (verse 39). Part of our sacrifice will also include our humility, our humbleness is our posture. Physically laying on the ground is one thing; physically being laid out before the Father should communicate something to Him but it needs to be combined and coupled with, in conjunction with, in concert with our emotional and our humility, our humbleness. We do not get physically out before God and still keep our pride in front of us; those cannot co-exist. Regardless of what position you are in, if you go before the Lord with pride as you pray, He cannot hear you anyway. I would not listen to you either. You are asking Him for the moon, the stars, and to give you the desires of your heart which is fine, but you ask with the 'You owe me' attitude, and in order for us to pray effectively, have a great relationship with Christ, be the child of God He calls us to be we have got to discard that personality trait anyway. It is not of God! Not to be used in front of God for that purpose, no, absolutely not. We have to abandon that behavior. When we are spiritual before God in a prostrate manner, He can see us and get us out of our own way. He can move those things out that encumber us and hinder us from being able to present ourselves to Him in the genuine fashion which He made us. Our destination is to be mentally, spiritually, emotionally and physically prostrate before the Lord.

Put your pride aside. What are you holding on to it for anyway? Do not let your pride reduce you so that you start asking why do you need God. You have got to get past some things, even some places, where you were not fulfilled even if you think you are blaming God for that lack of fulfillment. You have no idea why that was the best thing for you, and that is easy to say, but I am a witness. There are some things that I have been doing in my life, and I want to know so badly, what the real outcome of this is not to make myself feel better, but so I can understand that when God designed this life for me, "How is it that You came up with this particular decision?" It is really difficult for me to wrap my brain around at times but I certainly want to be able to get my life in line with the will of God. In order to do that, I have to get out of God's way.

The sacrifice of prayer involves your whole self, not the representative that you flash in front of the outside world but your whole, authentically, genuine self — even if you do not know who that is. Go prostrate before the Lord. Prepare for what God's will is for your life – prepare for what God's will is for your life. Years ago there was a bracelet, a theme, concerts, a concept that asked 'what would Jesus do' and we have these bracelets and T-shirts and scarves, arm bands, pencils, pens, sticky notes which read: 'what would Jesus do?' It was to urge us to continue to have the mind of Christ and to consider what would Christ do in our situation.

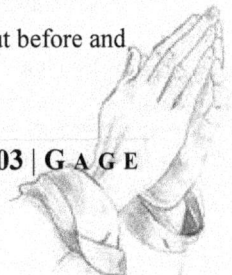

Now understand that Christ would not go to some of the places that we have struggle with, but what will He do for us, through us? What would He do if He were in our shoes? And the likelihood is that He would never be in some of the places where we would find ourselves in trouble in – if He is there, He is there to reach down and pull us out of that foolishness. You have to prepare mentally for what God's will is, and there is a process for preparing for God's will which is to understand what God's word says. Do you understand what God's word says? God's word is going to dictate your thought process. "Well God I want this to work so how will this affect my future? How many persons is this going to inconvenience, hurt, damage, harm? If you come up with a large number, the answer is no. As you consider your past, "What about this? What should I do with this? How will I handle this? If it did not work out before and you have not changed or grown up and matured since then, it will not work out again. We normally use the example of how you handle money. If you cannot handle $10, why would He give you $10 million? He also wants to know that if He gives you $10 million, are you going to give Him $1 million? Prepare for God's will in your life by asking Him: "Is this Your will? Is this Your will, Lord God? Is this Your will? Lord, let it be Your will." As you prepare for what God's will is for your life, be prepared to accept it, submit to it and carry it out even if you do not like it – even if you dislike it. You have to remind yourself that God's will overrides your perceived truth and desire. His will is going to override where you are mentally, spiritually – His will is going to override that and He is going to override it to the point where He says: "I need you to do this. I need you to be the spokesperson over here for that."

There are some things that I think God wants me to do. He puts me in a specific position to have the experience to be able to have the type of compassion and the knowledge that will help a whole group of people. If it is that I am supposed to go out and present on behalf of some people who have never had a voice before because I can be trusted to use my voice and that is why I am in this particular experience that I am in.

Number 1, I have got to submit to that. God is going to open up the doors to make those things transpire. God is going to give support to that situation and because He does that, His will be done. It is going to help the whole group of people who have never been served in this capacity before, but it is a very scary venture for me. I do not necessarily want just to go in and take care of this particular issue, and it is a social issue – I do not want to do it but it is about sacrifice. When you before the Father and say things like: "Lord, I would love to know Your will for my life." You have no idea what you have asked for but be prepared to find out.

In the process of studying God's word, being able to spend time with Him and listening to His voice, He is looking at us for elements around us that have some things in common – some common thread. You want to give the proper attention to that because you want to make sure that you do not overlook the things that God has for you. God wants us to have a particular posture of humility. Further, it is one of love, one of compassion, one where people figure that whatever they do is postured towards God, and whatever it is you do is purposed for God, when you pray you pray and carry out the will of God. Sometimes as we prepare for the will of God, the answer is going to be no and then there is a reason.

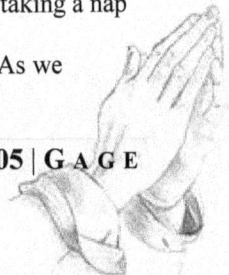

If I had fought against what I now know to be God's will then I might have died. The career that I was in the year before September 11 would have led me to New York, to the World Trade Centre on the trading floor on that day but instead I was asleep on the sofa expecting my first child. I was taking a nap before I was to go to work as a retail manager. Thy will be done. As we prepare for what God's will is and as we lay prostrate before Him, as we present what our truths are, there is a sacrifice when we pray. And sometimes we pray we might give up what it is we actually want for a greater cause – a greater thing – His will.

Lord God, afresh we thank You this day, for all that You have for us and everything that You would have for us to do, so Lord we pray Your choicest blessings over the desires of our hearts. And Lord allow them to be lined up with Your will and allow Your will to lined up with our hearts. And may we just ask You for those things that are in Your will and while they seem visibly impossible. Oh Lord God, we want to make sure that we give You the best of everything that we have as a piece of where we are headed.

We want to give ourselves fully to You as a sacrifice and pray that we will spend quality time with You in the morning and throughout the day Lord God, through our study and meditation, our witness, our service. So Lord God, we thank You afresh again for all that You allow for us to get done and accomplished even if it is not under Your umbrella.

It is in Your Son Jesus' name that I pray and ask these blessings.

Amen.

A Call to Pray

Philippians 1:3-11 (NIV)

Thanksgiving and Prayer

3 I thank my God every time I remember you. 4 In all my prayers for all of you, I
always pray with joy 5 because of your partnership in the gospel from the first
day until now, 6 being confident of this, that he who began a good work in you
will carry it on to completion until the day of Christ Jesus.

7 It is right for me to feel this way about all of you, since I have you in my
heart and, whether I am in chains or defending and confirming the gospel, all of
you share in God's grace with me. 8 God can testify how I long for all of you
with the affection of Christ Jesus.

9 And this is my prayer: that your love may abound more and more in knowledge
and depth of insight, 10 so that you may be able to discern what is best and may
be pure and blameless for the day of Christ, 11 filled with the fruit of
righteousness that comes through Jesus Christ—to the glory and praise of God.

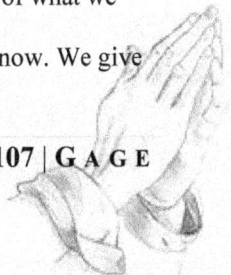

Lord God, how I bless You and thank You and love You on this day. Lord God, we thank You for this day. We have come together today Lord God to pray and to preach and praise You for what You do in our lives. Lord God, I thank You afresh right now because You are the God that we love, that we worship, that we cherish and that we honor. Lord God, we thank You right now for allowing us to be forgiven of our sins. We thank You for the gift of Your Son Jesus Christ, and we thank You for the gift of the Holy Spirit. Lord God right now afresh we thank You for giving us what we need, some of what we want, and for hearing our prayers. Lord God, we thank You right now. We give

You all the glory and honor. It is in Your Son, Jesus' name that we pray and ask these blessings. Amen.

A CALL TO PRAY

Paul is the author of just about half of the New Testament. When he authors these books, there is always a prayer. But this particular prayer is similar to a couple of other ones that are throughout the New Testament but I want to lift for your attention and understanding a few things about A Call to Pray. Verse 3 reads: "I thank my God every time I remember you." When you consider all of the things that are going on, the hustle and bustle that goes on just in your mind, in your heart and in your soul, the chaos. What do you do when God brings people to your remembrance? When a person comes to my remembrance, they show up. Within days of the thought of them, they show up, or they call, and they are present. And if God can drop a person in your spirit; if God can allow someone to cross your mind, do you not think at some point that person is worthy of your prayer?

I was at church when a lady passed by me and saw me and hugged me and was surprised to see me and was excited to see me and said you have been on my mind. I told her thank you, then I asked her to continue praying for me. I let her know that I loved her just like she loved me, but I had also been thinking about her. I had just written her name down in the study guide for persons that I would like to help me critique my course of study. And so, I wanted her to know that so I shared it with her.

When we think about people in the body of Christ and when we think about people who are not in the body of Christ, that is our first call to pray. Just because they crossed your mind. We want to be very clear about that because we are told to forgive one another, love one another, keep one another lifted in prayer, and to fellowship with other believers, then we are to pray. We want to do those things neither because we are commanded to do them, nor because it is the right thing to do, but because we want to, because we see the need to, and because of the benefit we see. We want to do that because the Holy Spirit does that for us.

Verses 4-6 reads: [4]"In all my prayers for all of you, I always pray with joy [5]because of your partnership in the gospel from the first day until now, [6]being confident of this, that he who began a good work in you will carry it on to completion until the day of Christ Jesus."

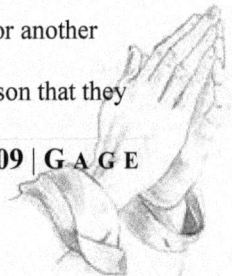

Our second call to prayer is our partnership with others. Paul is working an entire section of the globe; he is traveling. His prayer is that we do not get weak or weary in our well doing. Our prayer is that we do not burn out, that we are never tiring in our efforts and that we keep the faith. You are praying for another person to not give in to the struggle. You are praying for another person to not faint while working. You are praying for another person that they do not quit while we are doing what it is we are called to do. We are praying that what God will do for us and what God has going on for us, and what He wants us to do is something that we can continue on doing, with excellence. With that being said, why does there need to be a call to pray? Should we just do this naturally? Well, the answer is no, we are not just going to do it naturally. We are not going just to do it even though it seems like the right thing to do. Sometimes we have to be prompted in our call to pray. And there are many reasons why. One is sheer 'I did not know.' 'I do not know how to pray.' 'I do not feel comfortable praying for others.' 'I do not know what to pray for when I pray for others, but in our call to pray it is daily and regularly.' It is when that person crosses your mind, and it is in part because of the partnership that we have formed. Now, that partnership is designed to support each other in ministry. Support each other when we are going through our difficult times, to support each other when we stand in need of something, a hug, prayer, and other compassionate activities.

Verse 7 reads: "It is right for me to feel this way about all of you, since I have you in my heart and, whether I am in chains or defending and confirming the gospel, all of you share in God's grace with me."

The phrase I would like to lift out of this passage for you is 'since I have you in my heart.' What we want to understand about ministry is that it requires your heart. It requires more of who you are. Complete ministry requires more of who you are. And inside of that, you have to give it all you have. I love Paul for many reasons, and this scripture highlights one of the reasons why I love him the most: Paul gives his heart away. To us. And when he is giving his heart away, he is being used by God to show us a transparent, authentic love that others wish they had.

You have to get to a point where you understand that giving your heart to others is part of the work we do and it is being selfless and is very rewarding and completely fulfilling if we do it right. We have got to give that heart away without contention, without conditions, and without strings attached. When we do that, you can then say 'since I have you in my heart.' The most important part of Paul saying this is that you have taken a residency within his heart. You cannot move yourself out. It is a God-designed residency.

When you are residing in someone's heart and vice versa, someone is residing in your heart, they did not get there because of the decision the two of you made. They were placed there by God. So removal is not an option. Kicking someone out is not something you personally can do.

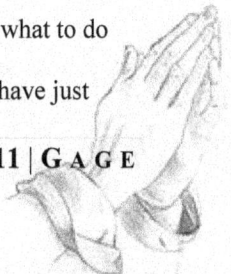

And there is a saying: two friends and they fall out, and they really try to be mad and over something simple, not something major, something simple. Well, because this person has taken up residence in your heart, you cannot just put them out. It was not your job. Now you are trying to figure out what to do because something that should have been rather simple, that could have just been avoided and talked about is now turned into something way too big to manage, because you have let too much stuff filter in and take root.

So, since I have you in my heart, because you are a part of me that is a call to pray. "God can testify how I long for all of you with the affection of Christ Jesus." A call to pray because I love you, with a Christ Jesus-defined love. Paul is one of those unique Christians who you know if he is on your side, then your life will never be the same. Paul is the reliable Christian. And you have got to give credit to Paul for knowing that he is that guy. Paul loves in such an authentic manner that he puts shame on those of us who are selfish. He unashamedly walks up and tells people that God can testify how I long for all of you with the affection of Christ Jesus. That is a profound scripture sentence. There are kids who grow up with the ability to refer us to others: 'if you don't believe me go ask such and such.' Inside of that statement, they make the other person the authority, they are the witness, they are the expert, and they are the guru. They are the person that knows, if you do not believe that I feel this way, go ask such and such.

But in this one sentence, he pulls the ultimate authority, coupled with the ultimate definition, Paul combines them to say if you do not believe I feel this way about you, ask God. God can and He will testify on my behalf how I long for all of you with a Christ Jesus-defined affection. I love you just like Christ loves you. And God can testify to it. That is a big deal. You see there are times when you will never say God can testify about how I feel about you because if God were to testify, He is going to tell the whole truth. God is going to disclose what you have never said aloud. He is going to give us the whole skinny, if you will. He is going to let you know that no she really does not feel like this, what she said and feels is x y and z and that might not be as favorable as you initially tried to present. But he is so serious and so committed, and his love is so confirmed for us, he says God can testify. And that is a call to pray.

First of all, we want to be able to feel like that about the people around us. They may not be with whom we serve at this time but potentially who will serve with us. We want to feel like that about people we see and come in contact with. Because we then can say to ourselves, this is why we do what we do. Our third call to pray is to be able to put our guard down. To be a part of being able to have someone in your heart and feel the kind of affection of Christ Jesus about someone is putting your guard down and allowing yourself to love the way Christ says we are supposed to and that we are able to. We are praying to have this level of love.

The call to prayer. Verse 9 reads: "And this is my prayer: that your love may abound more and more in knowledge and depth of insight."

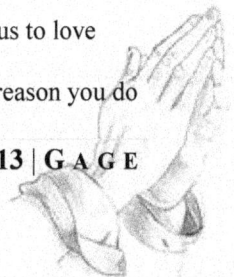

He wants our love to grow in our knowledge and our insight. And that knowledge and insight is Christ Jesus, the word of God. He wants us to love because we know more about Him. It is as if He is saying that the reason you do not love like I do was because you do not know Him like I do and I want you to love like I do and know Him like I do. A call to pray is going to be centered around the fact that our job is to know and love. I pray our Lord Savior Jesus Christ, but that love is not evident through Lord I love You. The love is evident through Lord I serve You through others. There is a scripture that says, how can I say I love You to a God I have never seen, but I cannot love the people that are in front of me. He says that is not of a balanced mind. Your words and deeds do not match. Prayer is supposed to be able to develop you in a place where you can love others more and more. Prayer enables you to look past the situation, and you can look past their frailties because you want to love them and take care of them at the level that Christ would have. You have to get to an intimacy with Christ that allows us to love other people unselfishly, and some of us have more work to do than others.

Verse 10 reads: "So that you may be able to discern what is best and may be pure and blameless for the day of Christ." If we have abounding love and more knowledge and depth of that insight and so that we may use that knowledge and depth of insight to discern what is best and may be pure and blameless until the day of Christ. We have to ask ourselves again, are we sensitive to the spirit of discernment. The spirit of discernment shares things with you that nobody else knows. It gives you the heads up that this is about to take place. It gives you time to prepare what it is that you need to prepare for.

Verse 11 reads: "Filled with the fruit of righteousness that comes through Jesus Christ—to the glory and praise of God. A Call to Pray. Paul puts a lot of language together but when you break down those three scripture verses because it is one sentence, it is easier to digest and use daily. He is praying for you to have more love, that your love may abound, and in the context of that love, he wants it to get past the boundary boxes you have set up for your love. Each of us has set up a boundary box and I would love to call it parenthetical or metaphorical, but no, there is a real box around our love and it is so that our boundaries are established and that is some new 21st century thing about this boundary thing. I have kept within my bounds and my limits. That is not acceptable to God. We cannot do that. We have to stop the limitations. We have got to stop it in such a manner that we do not continue to love within limits. Jesus Christ has asked us to love without limits and for our love to know no bounds but yet we still do, and we still do and we are fine with that. And it is not really ok. So we want to get to a place where we can love without that boundary box. He feels like our knowledge and insight, as well as a spirit of discernment, would allow us to do more loving, to be more loving and then we can be better disciples for Christ.

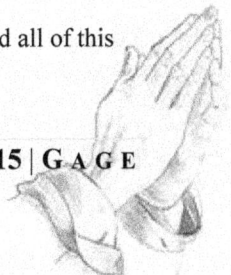

Here is what the fruit of righteousness means do the right thing, we are righteous and we do the right thing and we treat others well and we do what we are supposed to do. That righteousness comes from Christ Jesus and all of this goes to the praise and glory of God. A Call to Pray is also a call to action, the things we want to avoid doing. There are things we are responsible to take care of, things that we are going to be responsible for, and because we are going to be doing those things, this call to pray is important. We need to be able to answer God the first time when He calls upon us to love, discerning who to love, and who means us harm. We still have to love that person. Love people who do not seem loveable. Love people who do not love you back. That is all a part of a calling on our lives, and our call to pray is going to be one of those areas where we say this is what we are made of. This is what we are made to do. We have got to ask ourselves what is stopping us from answering our call to pray. What is stopping us from answering and doing the work? Paul makes it seem easy, and I envy that from time to time. But he and Jesus had a conversation on the road to Damascus. That is a powerful enough dialogue to do whatever Paul says. It may be that you are just avoiding that dialogue, where God calls you into submission unto Him and with that being said, we have to understand our calling to be able to answer. It is a call to pray. Amen.

Lord God, how we thank You and love You this day for what You reveal to us as the calling on our lives to pray, to love, to hold people in our hearts, and to long for them with the affection of Christ Jesus. Lord, I thank You right now for what You have revealed in this word today. Lord God, we thank You right now for Your message, and we thank You for your messenger.

Undergird me, keep me strengthened, keep me reminded of what my calling is on my life, and Lord God, I just thank You right now because You are God and God alone. You are going to do for us only what You designed. So Lord, I thank You afresh for who You are to me and how You call me in to service for You. Thank You for trusting me with my assignments. It is in Jesus' name that I pray and ask Your blessings, Amen. Thank God.

The Transparency of Prayer

Colossians 1:3-14 (NIV)

Thanksgiving and Prayer

3 We always thank God, the Father of our Lord Jesus Christ, when we pray for you, 4 because we have heard of your faith in Christ Jesus and of the love you have for all God's people— 5 the faith and love that spring from the hope stored up for you in heaven and about which you have already heard in the true message of the gospel 6 that has come to you. In the same way, the gospel is bearing fruit and growing throughout the whole world—just as it has been doing among you since the day you heard it and truly understood God's grace. 7 You learned it from Epaphras, our dear fellow servant, who is a faithful minister of Christ on our[b] behalf, 8 and who also told us of your love in the Spirit.

9 For this reason, since the day we heard about you, we have not stopped praying for you. We continually ask God to fill you with the knowledge of his will through all the wisdom and understanding that the Spirit gives,[c] 10 so that you may live a life worthy of the Lord and please him in every way: bearing fruit in every good work, growing in the knowledge of God, 11 being strengthened with all power according to his glorious might so that you may have great endurance and patience, 12 and giving joyful thanks to the Father, who has qualified you to share in the inheritance of his holy people in the kingdom of light. 13 For he has rescued us from the dominion of darkness and brought us into the kingdom of the Son he loves, 14 in whom we have redemption, the forgiveness of sins.

Lord, how we bless You on this day, thank You on this day. We thank You Lord God on this hour that You have given us an opportunity to come before You again and hear a word from You lord God. We thank You right now that you are going to give us exactly what it is that You have for us and exactly what we should want for us to know and use immediately this day. Lord God, we thank You right now for the forgiveness of our sins, for the redemption of our sins by Your son Jesus Christ in burial and resurrection. Lord God, we thank You right now for who will hear this message and who will be touched and enhanced by being reached by such outpouring. Lord God, we thank You right now for using and calling me. Thank You for enhancing and encouraging me. Lord God, we thank You right now in Your Son Jesus's name. We pray and ask these blessings in His name.

THE TRANSPARENCY OF PRAYER

The book of Colossians is written by an apostle named Paul. Paul, an apostle of Jesus Christ by the will of God, comes with Timothy to the church of Colossus. Paul has been on a preaching tour, if you will. He has taken the gospel around to many and Paul is unique in his ministry because initially he was against Christ, and openly so. Because he was openly against Christ, he was able to be used openly to be with Jesus Christ. He openly was against, and now he can openly be for Jesus. Paul's mission is to preach the gospel. Paul's calling leads him to places where he may not have known, but where Christ needs to be known, because of Paul's obedience, Paul leaves and Jesus is now known. Initially, as he is preaching, they will ask, 'Wasn't he the one who spoke against Christ?' But because of his vicious reputation, I do not recall anyone daring to ask him that face-to-face.

You take a person who was against Christ, who was turned around to preaching for Christ in the span of ten days. From getting his attention on the road, causing him to be blind, sending Adonys, giving him his instructions, training him in the ways of Christ, and the preaching training took ten days. Again that was my calculation based on the verbiage in Acts 9. However, I want us to be clear on however long it was, it was shorter than what we ever do, and the time that we take in deciding whether or not we want to follow the directions that Christ gives us.

Going further and making sure we understand each other, we have an opportunity to be transparent. Paul gives us an example, and he is forever interceding. Forever interceding on our behalf. He is ensuring that we have the benefits of Jesus and the Holy Spirit. He's not going to let us out without knowing prayer.

When I did my study of Paul, I considered the fact that he opens each book praying, and he prays during each book. At least one time in each book he is going to pray. That lets us know that, number one: prayer is important. Prayer is important to Christ and to God; there has been this ongoing conversation.

The second thing, though, is what happens in your prayer. This is a very important piece of our message; we have to figure out how to pray without the mask. Paul is an example of many things, and prayer is our focus. Inside of him being our example of many things and prayer being the most important, inside of that prayer, he teaches us some things. He teaches us some very important things.

First, he teaches us that we are to encourage one another. We are to encourage one another. He opens this prayer with [3]We always thank God, the Father of our Lord Jesus Christ, when we pray for you, [4]because we have heard of your faith in Christ Jesus and of the love you have for all God's people— [5]the faith and love that spring from the hope stored up for you in heaven and about which you have already heard in the true message of the gospel [6]that has come to you.

He encourages you. He seeks out what is good, and he capitalizes on that. He reinforces that. He presents it with a sense of urgency that this is what we are supposed to do to one another. We are supposed to enhance and upgrade and undergird one another, and the only way to do that is going to be the fact that we encourage one another. It is by no chance; it is not by happenstance that he comes to these churches, and he gives to each church a prayer. He gives to each church an opportunity to understand prayer. He says to them, beyond a shadow of a doubt, with unequivocal boldness, full sobriety, and directly, we pray for you. We always pray for you. We thank God for you; we thank God for who you are.

His role is to instruct. His role is to preach. His role is to correct. His role is to chastise and chide. He is going to use the word of God to let them know what it is that makes them excellent and what it is they may not have done well. He is so open in praying and encouragement. He wants to share that with everyone.

Now, as he encourages them, he also informs. As Paul informs, he goes on with, "In the same way, the gospel is bearing fruit and growing throughout the whole world—just as it has been doing among you since the day you heard it and truly understood God's grace."

Paul continued to share, [7]You learned it from Epaphras, our dear fellow servant, who is a faithful minister of Christ on our behalf, [8]and who also told us of your love in the Spirit.

We want to be clear that fruit is present. Bearing fruit is possible. Bearing fruit has its place. It is not something that we want to think is for somebody else. Bearing fruit is for us. We have to bear fruit because others are expecting it of us. We have to bear fruit because others are expecting it of us. We need to consider the fruit because it is the fruit that gives glory and honor to God and evidence of God.

Paul wants us to make sure that we understand why we are called. Paul gives us information on why we are here. He leads by example. He prays. He instructs. He teaches. He answers questions. He puts people's mind at rest. Nowhere in here does he tear up the church. He does not do things that are not of God. He does not cause a big church fight and a battle and walk off the stage.

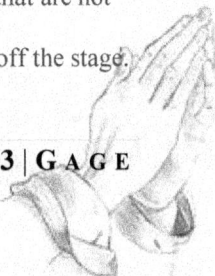

He does not do that. He is going to give you exactly what you need to go forward in excellence.

As you go forward in excellence, prayer is your first tool. If we are going to be the people that we are supposed to be, we have got to do some things differently. Part of that doing something different is a transparent prayer life. We cannot allow ourselves to think that we are praying authentically when clearly we are not. We cannot feel like we are praying authentically when clearly, we are not. We are not doing anyone a favor by saying the standard, perfunctory prayer, and whatever we think God wants to hear. We are not doing ourselves or God any favors.

First of all, if we do not pray authentically and tell God exactly what is on our mind and what is worrying us, we have committed a sin because we are lying. We are lying, and those lies are not things we want to perpetuate in any state, form, or fashion. When we enter prayer time, it is time to tell God the real deal, the skinny. Whatever you want to call it, because number one, He already knows. Number two, He really wants to know if you are willing to tell yourself the truth. The only person who is hurt by those lies is you. You cannot go forward if you continue to lie. He cannot answer you if you continue to lie because you will not be able to hear Him because you are in your own mind believing one thing when something different totally is true. We want to get to a place in our lives where we do not have to do that anymore. You see, Paul prays transparently.

He lets you know where the truth is. [10] so that you may live a life worthy of the Lord and please him in every way: bearing fruit in every good work, growing in the knowledge of God, [11] being strengthened with all power according to his glorious might so that you may have great endurance and patience, [12] and giving joyful thanks to the Father, who has qualified you to share in the inheritance of his holy people in the kingdom of light.

We cannot go into those places lying. We cannot go in those places lying because He is there. We cannot go in those places thinking that we know but clearly that we do not. We cannot go into those places still bruised, battered, broken, hurting, refusing to heal, refusing to get help, refusing to seek amends and reconciliation. We cannot go into those places still refusing to come clean with God. We cannot go into those places like that, yet we do it every day – at least we try! We try this every day. We get up every day and say, "Lord, today is great, and You are worthy to be praised," and then the first person comes to us, and we growl and we bark and we are vicious, and then we are hurtful. But the Lord is great, and He is good. I love those Christians that you walk up to, and they tell you, "I am blessed and highly favored by the Lord." I am asking myself: are you saying that because it is what you believe it or until you believe it? Who are we looking at this to be believed by? Who are you hoping believes this?

I agree, the Lord is blessing you and you are highly favored but there are some people that walk up to you and ask how you are doing, and you ought tell them, “I am not fine, and right now I need prayer, and I want you to pray for me right now.” And the other person ought to be okay with that. There is a transparency in prayer that we lack, and because we lack it and we are standing in our own way of what we could be potentially blessed with if we would just be strong enough to tell the truth.

Lord, I made a mistake. I should not have done that. I should not have run out in the street in front of that woman. I should not have done that. I should not have told her the way I really felt in that setting, with that tone of voice, with those words I used. It was not that I should not have told her how I felt; it was that I did not want to recklessly hurt another child of God with an intention. We always want to leave that part out, the “with intention” part - we want to leave that out. But if we feel like we are telling the truth in love, and actually, no you are not! You told the truth, and you told it the way you wanted to tell it. You intended to get her attention and tell you what you thought of what she did, but you do not go and ask for forgiveness and talk about that with God with the transparency it deserves.

The transparency that we are looking for, as well, is to be able to be authentic with ourselves. It is preventing us; our lack of authenticity with ourselves is preventing us from being authentic with God. It is preventing it. It is not something that we can do very well. Some days we can be transparent, but some days we wear the mask, we put it on, and we lock it on tight. We can shake it, and it is not going to come off. You cannot even tell; we have a seamless color. It is better than our makeup foundation, for men who do not know what foundation is, it is that color we put on our faces and it looks just like our face but it makes our skin look very smooth. We put that mask on, maybe the mask is clear, who knows? But what we do know is this: we hide behind it. We cloak things behind it, and prayer is not a place for that. Prayer ought to be the place where you can walk in, to the richness of Jesus Christ, the fullness and the fullest measure of God. In prayer, we will put our stuff down, not at the hands of another but at the hands of God, at the foot of God, at the heart of God, and in God's hands. You are going to put your entire burden of your divorce, your marriage, your children, your education, your finances, the fact that your dreams have been crushed and broken, the fact that your parents have hurt you, the fact that somebody else has hurt you, the fact that you are seeking healing, and you want to be healed in God's hands transparently in prayer.

Matthew 26 shares that Jesus laid out on the ground in front of God in order to be able to lay completely prostrate. All in all, we have to be transparent, and it starts with ourselves. I have told people often that I would like to eventually get married again, and I want to be able to marry someone who already knows me and loves me right now, and I say this at the end: I just want a nice, comfortable place to put my stuff down. And by stuff I mean: the stuff, your junk, your baggage, your hurts, your ails, your pains, your whatever - but here is the problem. How am I going to put it down in front of a human man, a human, and I cannot put it down in front of my Lord and Savior, Jesus Christ?

You want someone else to handle your things, but you will not give them over to God. And why is that? You have to be able to hand over who you are, completely surrender it back to the God, who loves you, who created you, who knows you! And who wants the best for you, without prejudice, without issue.

That is who you want. We give ourselves over to others whom we cannot trust, who loves us conditionally for as long as the time allows. We have to get past that point. We have to get to a different place. That different place has its value, and its value is going to upgrade your value. Being able to be transparent, completely free, telling the whole truth, and nothing but the truth even though it is going to hurt sometimes, sometimes it is going to offend, and sometimes it will cause pain even to someone else. It is going to free you up to be a whole you. You are going to wonder what happened to parts of yourself; it is because there is no transparency in anything you do. We have to get to a better point, where we can be transparent with the God that created us that knows us that loves us anyway. He already knows what you did, He already knows that. He already knows what you did not do. As a matter of fact: He knew it before you did it. He knew you were going to do it. How are we going to become more transparent?

Decide that you are going to stop being fake with yourself, start with yourself. Ask God to help you give Him what is, He is owed, what is due to Him by being able to share with Him transparently what is going on. Try to figure out why it is that you are so taken with not being able to say those things out loud because here is the thing: if you cannot say it out loud, then you probably should not have done it.

We need to think through all the steps, the consequences of our actions; we need to consider them more carefully as we move ahead. We need to look at our behavior and think about our behavior from the point of: if I do this today, how long and how far are the effects that are the consequences of this? You realize that our sins costs generations to come, three and four generations out—people who will not even know you are going to be pained by your sin and paying for your sin because they are the consequences of your behavior. We want to get to a point in our lives where we stop costing them so much. I am not worried about spending my social security right now; I am worried about those sins that are going to cost me later. I do not want my child to pay for what their great-grandparents did, someone they might never lay eyes on costs them some repercussions in the future. This is not the kind of pay-it-forward that we were talking about!

Transparency and prayer require that you put the gauntlet down, put your unforgiveness aside, put the lack of the ability to reconcile with others put it in the garbage and come forward knowing that you are able to overcome that which displeases God. Transparency is worth it. God will meet there. Trust and believe. Why otherwise would God honor the man who is up and down the road, blaspheming and talking bad about Him? Accusing Him, talking against the Lord, and now he is the author of 50% of the New Testament because he came forward and said: This is a privilege of following my lord and Savior Jesus Christ, and I am going to be transparent. That is why Paul was picked, because he could be trusted to be transparent in his prayer time. If I were just to get to the ability of transparency and a point of authenticity with God, then I can be blessed. It behooves us to get there and get that quickly and swiftly. It is worth it. The value is overwhelmingly profitable for you.

Amen.

Lord God, I thank You for this time, and we thank You for being able to be transparent before You. Lord, I thank You for the gift of prayer and the power that prayer offers. Lord God, thank You for being able to approach Your throne of grace with openness and honesty.

Lord God, I thank You for the wisdom to pray. Lord God, thank You for the gift for Holy Spirit, who intercedes on my behalf. Lord God, thank You for the lives that this touches and vessel You chose to deliver it.

Master, thank You for loving me, in spite of my less than great behavior. I love You. I pray this prayer and these blessings in Jesus' name. Amen.

With Some Enlightened Company

Romans 8:26-27 (NIV)

26 In the same way, the Spirit helps us in our weakness. We do not know what
we ought to pray for, but the Spirit himself intercedes for us through wordless
groans. 27 And he who searches our hearts knows the mind of the Spirit, because
the Spirit intercedes for God's people in accordance with the will of God.

Lord God, I thank You right now afresh for being able to serve You in this manner. Thank You for this gift of teaching, preaching, and intercession, as well as encouragement. Lord, I thank You right now for doing only what You can do, only what You can do, and exercise the power that You have within You. Lord God for You being God and God alone and showing me what You have me to do, have me to go, want me to be and be effective in the places where I am assigned. This prayer I pray in Your Son Jesus' name and I pray that You forgive me of all my sins and that You help me forgive all who have sinned against me. It is in Your Son Jesus' name I pray and ask His blessings. Amen.

WITH SOME ENLIGHTENED COMPANY

The definition of enlighten as a verb is to give intellectual or spiritual light to something, instruct, impart knowledge to. That comes from dictionary.com, and I will say it again: to give intellectual and spiritual light, to instruct, to impart knowledge to. Now this company that we are talking about is the Holy Spirit and the Holy Spirit is the third part of the Trinity. There is God, Jesus Christ, and the Holy Spirit.

The Holy Spirit was left for us by Jesus. In John 14 verse 26, "but the Counselor, the Holy Spirit whom the Father will send in my name will teach You all things and remind You of everything I have said to You." And so He leaves us the Holy Spirit. A gift for us. John 14 verse 6 says, and I will ask the Father, and He will give you another Counselor to be with you forever, the spirit of truth. The world cannot accept Him because it neither sees Him or knows Him, but you know Him for He lives with you and will be in you. As you consider the fact that the Holy Spirit was a gift for us to live with us and dwelling of us, so we consider those things, you have to ask yourself, what is this Holy Spirit. What is this Holy Spirit?

So verse 26 of Romans 8 reads, "in the same way the spirit helps us in our weaknesses." Now when you talk about being enlightened, to be able to impart knowledge to give intellect or spiritual light to or instruct. First, we know that the Spirit is knowledgeable. And knowledgeable in all things as it relates to each of us according to what God wants us to have, be, and do. Well, why do you say that? Well, He is knowledgeable because in order to know what our weaknesses are, He have to be knowledgeable of us and He would have to be knowledgeable of God. In order to make that happen, you have to know what those weaknesses are and you have to know how to comfort us during that time of weakness. When He sent us the Holy Spirit, He sent someone to comfort us, that was one of the jobs of the Holy Spirit in order to know when to comfort us, how to comfort us, the best mechanism by which to comfort us, you have to have knowledge of the Father, of our Father God. He is not your best friend. See your best friend has knowledge of how to comfort you but it might not be prudent for the body. We all have a "go-to." We all have something that we go to when we do not have a good day or when we are not having something go our way or when we are having a hard time. For some of us it might be shopping. For some of us alcohol. For some it might be other things. Whatever that is, you have a go to and your best friends says 'well if it will you make you feel better, let's do such and such.' Well the Spirit wants to make you feel better, but only with the knowledge, and only within the will of God. That is the way that the Holy Spirit wants you to feel better. Nothing else is going to work, nothing else is going to be in the will of God.

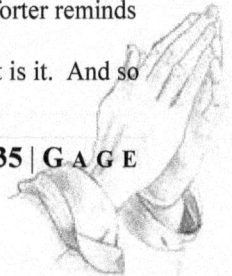

And so in order to be able to do that, He has got to be able to be knowledgeable. He also has to have the ability to be comforting. It cannot be a situation where He wants to be, but He is not comforting. He is there and designed to help us in our weakness. While in our weakness, one of the ways to help us is to allow the weakness to go away or if the weakness cannot go away, how to weather that particular storm, and maintain who we are through that weakness. Part of that particular process is going to involve being able to give ourselves diligently over to God because we are weak that is when He is strongest. So the whole goal is to make sure that we understand this is the way, one way of God getting our attention and keeping it. So that Comforter reminds us that we are God's and God's alone. We belong to Him and that is it. And so when the Holy Spirit comes to help us in our weakness, it is at the offering of God. He was sent by God, the Holy Spirit is sent, developed, created, fueled, undergirded, driven and led by God. The Holy Spirit is not acting on His own. It is under the complete instruction of the Lord, our God. So what we want to be sure of is that our God is going to be able to say to us, "We intend for you to have everything that We want you to have but in part of that is going to be if it be God's will." The Holy Spirit is only going to be able to do that. So, those weaknesses may not come out the way we want or the way we self-design, the way we proclaim. It is going to be one where we design this whole situation in a method where we can say Lord our God afresh we thank You for the Holy Spirit. We thank You right now for what it is that the Holy Spirit is able to give to us. The Holy Spirit only does the will of God. So some of those weaknesses are not just going to go away because we said so or because we say that the Holy Spirit is going to take care of everything. It may not be the way we want. We have just discerned that it is the Holy Spirit is knowledgeable, is going to do exactly what He says, according to whatever the Lord says for Him to do for us. Likewise, the Holy Spirit was sent to intercede on our behalf. Intercede, well yes. Intercede.

Intercession is when I stand in your place, I intercede on your behalf. An intercessory prayer is when I pray for you in a special, fervent way. Intercessors are normally gifted prayers. They pray with a fervency and a zeal, and a zest that only can come from being gifted by God to be able to pray.

Intercessors are people who we know and can count on who will pray on your behalf. It is almost written across their bodies: their demeanor, their face, their attitude, and their fervency. They can be seen praying regularly caught, if you will, praying. Well verse 26b says, "We do not know what we ought to pray for, but the Holy Spirit himself intercedes for us the groans that words cannot express."

Paul shares with us right there that there is going to be times when we do not know what to pray for. We get mixed up on our words, we do not know how to express how we feel, and we do not know how to express what is on our mind. There are times and days when the situation is so overwhelming, we are speechless. It will render silence for even the most gregarious individual. I for one can attest to that. There are going to be things in your life that do that. However, you want to be sure that you understand that there is an intercessor, when we do not know what to pray for, we can still go before the Father, our Lord, our God, our Rock, our Redeemer and say without a shadow of a doubt, Lord help me pray to You through what is happening to me as the Holy Spirit is going to do just that. The Holy Spirit is going to say I got this; I got this one. We do not know what we ought to pray for, but the Spirit Himself will intercede on our behalf with groans that words cannot express.

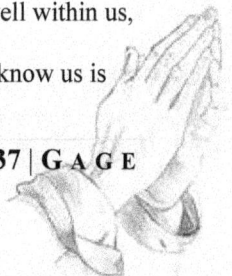

In order that the Holy Spirit be able to intercede again, the Holy Spirit has to be knowledgeable. The Holy Spirit's job is to indwell, to dwell within us, to live inside of us, to occupy the same space. In order for Him to know us is because He is inside of us. Now note to self, if the Holy Spirit is inside of us, just ask onesself what do I expose the Holy Spirit to. What good do I expose the Holy Spirit to? And what things should require some attention that I am not, should not be exposing the Holy Spirit to. We have got to be conscious of that, here is why. We have got to put ourselves in a whole different situation. You see the Holy Spirit shares this body with you so the thoughts you think, the Holy Spirit already knows, the heartbreak you feel the Holy Spirit already knows. The physical pain you are in the Holy Spirit already knows. What you have done to your body, the Holy Spirit already knows. When you have negative thoughts, the Holy Spirit is aware. When you have things that disturb you, the Holy Spirit was made aware first. Even before you told your best friends. When you are anxious, the Holy Spirit knows. When you are burdened, the Holy Spirit knows.

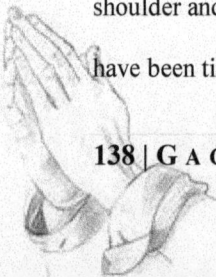

So what we have to understand that the Holy Spirit is aware and so it is not any surprise when you cannot pray, when you cannot figure out what to say, but you are bold enough and wise enough, fearful of God enough to go before the Father and say Lord, I just do not know what to even say I want to pray to You Lord God, but I do not have any words right now Holy Spirit. I do not even think we need to ask, I do not even think we need to prompt the spirit however I believe that He just jumps in there and says it is My turn. He taps you on the shoulder and says I got this. He goes before the Father on our behalf. And there have been times I believe that He has gone before the Father, without you even knowing. Without you having any knowledge that this is has taken place. But He has gone on before you to say Lord God afresh we thank You and has been able to say some things to the Lord that You had not thought of that You were unable to verbalize that you could not imagine and or think and he is done exactly that upfront in advance ahead of time.

And so we have to give the Holy Spirit what is due and what belongs to the Holy Spirit. And that is the attention that the Holy Spirit also deserves. There is a whole lot of work involved in being the Holy Spirit. We have got to recognize that, that is very important, extremely critical.

Now verse 27 reads [27] "And he who searches our hearts knows the mind of the Spirit, because the Spirit intercedes for God's people in accordance with the will of God. He who serves our hearts knows the mind of the Spirit." So when you talk about the fact that the mind of the Spirit and the mind of Christ and the mind of God are all the same, the Spirit is not going to do things that are not inline and aligned with God. It is not possible. The Holy Spirit is never going to second guess or challenge the will of God or the knowledge of God.

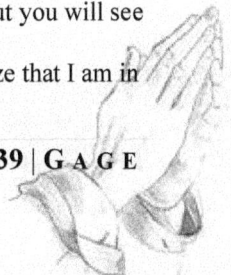

John 14:17-31 (NIV) reads [17] the Spirit of truth. The world cannot accept him, because it neither sees him nor knows him. But you know him, for he lives with you and will be in you. [18] I will not leave you as orphans; I will come to you. [19] Before long, the world will not see me anymore, but you will see me. Because I live, you also will live. [20] On that day you will realize that I am in

my Father, and you are in me, and I am in you. 21 Whoever has my commands
and keeps them is the one who loves me. The one who loves me will be loved by
my Father, and I too will love them and show myself to them."

22 Then Judas (not Judas Iscariot) said, "But, Lord, why do you intend
to show yourself to us and not to the world?"

23 Jesus replied, "Anyone who loves me will obey my teaching. My
Father will love them, and we will come to them and make our home with them.
24 Anyone who does not love me will not obey my teaching. These words you
hear are not my own; they belong to the Father who sent me.

25 "All this I have spoken while still with you. 26 But the Advocate, the
Holy Spirit, whom the Father will send in my name, will teach you all things
and will remind you of everything I have said to you. 27 Peace I leave with you;
my peace I give you. I do not give to you as the world gives. Do not let your
hearts be troubled and do not be afraid.

28 "You heard me say, 'I am going away and I am coming back to you.'
If you loved me, you would be glad that I am going to the Father, for the Father
is greater than I. 29 I have told you now before it happens, so that when it does
happen you will believe. 30 I will not say much more to you, for the prince of
this world is coming. He has no hold over me, 31 but he comes so that the world
may learn that I love the Father and do exactly what my Father has commanded
me.

Now let us understand how that is part of the Holy Spirit. That is the Holy Spirit and why the Holy Spirit can search us and know us.

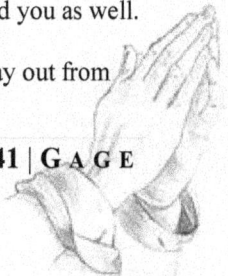

When you consider the fact that the Holy Spirit searches our hearts and knows the mind of the Spirit. If you are inside of something, suppose you are wearing a shirt and that shirt is made of Egyptian cotton where the seams are sewn down and is tagless. The cotton is so soft and so smooth that you just love getting inside of that shirt. It feels good against your skin so that you do not want to wear a camisole or an undershirt. It is smooth. It keeps you cool and does all these things because it is a certain type of cotton. This certain type of cotton is designed to do that and it feels so good. Now the opposite of that, let us talk about a shirt that has a tag that scratches your neck. It is straight out of the package. It has never been washed or ironed or treated at the dry cleaners. It is just out of a box. It may be a poly cotton blend that is going to stretch. The seams are not sewn down. And every time you turn, something scratches you. It is uncomfortable to be in that shirt. Well likewise let's look at the Holy Spirit. The Holy Spirit lives in some of us; all of us whom are Christians but understand that we are sometimes, we create an uncomfortability. It is not going to be comfortable to be inside of our bodies. We know that it is uncomfortable inside of our bodies because sometimes it is uncomfortable just to be in your presence on the outside of your body. Sometimes you do not even like to be in the presence of yourself. Honestly, it is hard for others to be around you as well. So let us understand that the Holy Spirit dwells there, day in and day out from this morning to the next morning. As the song says from the rising of the sun to the going down of the same, the Holy Spirit lives there. Have we ever considered as the Holy Spirit searches our heart, and as the Holy Spirit does His work, as the Holy Spirit gives us the will of God, as the Holy Spirit intercedes on our behalf, is there any way that we can make it easier on the Holy Spirit by giving Him some place pleasant to dwell? Now I say that very cautiously because there are times when we are not pleasant. There are times when we cannot overcome our own selves. There are times when we just cannot figure out how to be kind or pleasant or nice or forgiving or gracious or understanding or compassionate, there are just times when we cannot understand how to be nice and forgiving and forgetful. We cannot figure out how to do more and get nothing in return. We cannot figure that out, now can we?

There are times when my son says to my daughter she is a rude and meanie pants. Well initially that was really cute, I thought it was funny, I laughed and laughed. But his perception of her is that she does not treat him well. But she loves him dearly. She loves him more than what he will ever understand or comprehend. She is always defending him, looking out for him, helping him and not letting him get in any trouble. Yet he felt, even in all of her efforts, that she is a rude, meanie pants. Does the Holy Spirit feel like that in some of us as He dwells there? Does He feel like that sometimes that we are rude, meanie pants and there is nothing that we can do to be nice or kind to another individual? We have got to get ourselves at a point where it is not hard to search because it is not so much garbage in there. It is not so hard to intercede on our behalf because there is not so much self—inflicted tragedy.

Now lastly, we talked about this knowledgeable Holy Spirit. The Holy Spirit is only going to intercede in accordance to God's will. That means the Holy Spirit knows us. Searches our hearts and understands us. The Holy Spirit knows the will of God which means He also knows God's heart and all that God allows Him to know about Himself. What that means is that we have to accept what the Holy Spirit says is the will of God without complaint. We likewise should not question the Holy Spirit. It is not wise. It is not prudent. It is not timely. And it really has no place. We can talk about what we want, but we have no place to question because all that the Spirit does is follow the will of God. The Holy Spirit and Jesus Christ are the only two persons that can follow the will of God to the letter. We spend all of our time trying to know it. But we want to make sure that we know the part that resembles the will of God.

John 16:13-16 (NIV) reads [13] But when He, the Spirit of truth, comes,
He will guide you into all the truth. He will not speak on His own; He will speak
only what He hears, and He will tell you what is yet to come. [14] He will glorify
Me because it is from Me that He will receive what He will make known to you.
[15] All that belongs to the Father is mine. That is why I said the Spirit will receive
from Me what He will make known to you." [16] Jesus went on to say, "In a little
while you will see Me no more, and then after a little while you will see Me."

So understand that the Holy Spirit is going to do His job, strictly by the book, by the letter of the will of God. We have to be really careful to honor that. So at the same time, we have this Intercessor, this knowledgeable Intercessor who knows and will completely comply with the will of God—the Holy Spirit.

When I gave you the definition of enlightened, part of that definition was to instruct. He is referred to as a teacher in John chapter 14, verse 26, which reads, 'But the Advocate, the Holy Spirit, whom the Father will send in my name, will teach you all things and will remind you of everything I have said to you.' To give spiritual guidance to the knowledge of the will of God. And to be able to take that which is Jesus Christ and give it to us which is to impart knowledge. With some enlightened company is much responsibility. And the Spirit wants to give us His best which comes from God and gives us His best which He is gifted to give to us from God.

We have to become enlightened company. We have to appreciate His enlightenment. We have to go forward seeking to be enlightened by the Holy Spirit. We need to seek the Holy Spirit and ask for the Holy Spirit to guide me through this situation and negotiate this for me. Let me walk with You, Lord God so that I can understand what me to do and why You have me headed there. But more importantly that You are able to get the honor and the glory of all these things. With some enlightened company and when the Holy Spirit enlightens us, let us be the first ones for the very first time in our lives that just submits and accepts it without a word back. I tell my son all the time that there are some times I wish he would just say 'yes ma'am.' Likewise we should just say 'Yes Sir, God.' You want to make sure that you spend the proper time on exactly what God wants you to do. Follow His directions. Let Him guide you sometimes until it gets comfortable for you and then you can let Him guide you all the time.

The scripture says 'God will fight my battles if I just be still,' Exodus chapter 14, verse 14. I believe if I am still, He will fight my battles. It is indeed a privilege for Him to do so. And it is an outstanding position to be in when you are still and let Him fight your battles, when He sends you to war with the proper equipment and you come out the victor with no effort of your own, no planning of your own, no strategy of your own, nothing of your own that you chose; that you simply follow the will of God. Straight to battle and straight to victory! No detour, no side shows, no risk, no waiting, none of those things. If I would just be still, You will fight my battles. Some of us have to learn how to be still and make it pleasant for the Holy Spirit to dwell in you. Some of us are cantankerous on purpose. Is there any way we can change or rectify or modify those character traits so that we could be able to be easily indwelled by the Holy Spirit in a pleasant nature and able to be so pleasantly that we can hear Him on the first try so He does not have to talk loud or get out the bullhorn or anything like that? Amen.

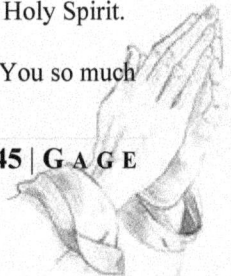

Thank You for Enlightened Company. Thank You for the Holy Spirit. Lord God, I thank You afresh for what You do in our lives. Thank You so much

Lord God for what You do within this vessel. Lord, I thank You for the lives where You use me to assist You with love and growth to prayer, to love, to help them change, to grow stronger, to grow wiser, to grow fit for ministry, to grow, to grow, and grow! Lord, I thank You for those who You place in front of me, for whom I model, who I follow, who I take into consideration. So Lord, I thank You right now afresh for doing all that You do. Especially, all that You do through and for me. Lord God, I thank You right now for what You are going to do in our lives, for our finances, for our homes, for our children, for our careers, for the ministry you allow us to take part in, and participate in. It is in Your Son Jesus' name that I pray and thank You for Your blessings.

Amen.

A Special Prayer Request

2 Thessalonians 3:1-5 (NIV)

Request for Prayer

3 As for other matters, brothers and sisters, pray for us that the message of the
Lord may spread rapidly and be honored, just as it was with you. 2 And pray that
we may be delivered from wicked and evil people, for not everyone has
faith. 3 But the Lord is faithful, and he will strengthen you and protect you from
the evil one. 4 We have confidence in the Lord that you are doing and will
continue to do the things we command. 5 May the Lord direct your hearts into
God's love and Christ's perseverance.

Lord God, how we love You and thank You and appreciate You for the gift of prayer. The instructions regarding prayer and the ability to pray without ceasing. Without reserve, without any type of heavy spirit, Lord, we thank You that You allow us to come before You with an intercessor that is not a human intercessor, without going to another person, without the requirement and permission of someone. Lord, we thank You for being able to be authentic in our prayers that we ask of You knowing that You love us and care for us, knowing that You are consumed with what we are and our well-being because You are our creator. Lord God, we thank You right now afresh for what You are going to do, what You have done, and what You are going to do in our lives. We thank You right now for this time, this vessel. Lord, we thank You again for Paul, there is absolutely no way to thank You enough for sending such a man to us and to give what You have given through Him to us. Oh Lord, we thank You right now, in Jesus name we pray. Amen.

A SPECIAL PRAYER REQUEST

First of all, the book of Thessalonians, 1st and 2nd are both written by Paul. Paul is traveling to churches to preach the gospel and at this time Paul takes Silas and Timothy along with him because the Thessalonians are in need of some assistance. Paul prays in each book that he has written in the New Testament. In this particular one, 2nd Thessalonians, he prays a prayer of thanksgiving then he requests prayer for himself and his traveling preachers, Timothy and Silas. When Paul is requesting prayer, it is not any different from when we request prayer, however when the prayer warrior needs prayer or requests prayer, that lets you know this is not something just to do. This is not something that we want to not give a proper credit to, to give the proper attention to. We want to understand that we know that the Lord our God has given us the ability to pray and given us the ability to do things in a fashion that pleases Him. And so at this time, Paul asks for prayer so I call our time that we are spending together "A Special Prayer Request" because Paul is asking for prayer, now let us see what it is that Paul is actually wants.

So as we consider our text, 'finally brothers pray for us that the message of the Lord may spread rapidly and be honored, just as it was with you.' The first thing that Paul shares with us is that this is the message of the Lord. Paul is not asking to be edified. Paul is not asking to be praised or glorified. Paul is asking that the message of the Lord be honored. And spread rapidly. Now, understand that there is going to be a method for this because again Paul is the author of this.

He asks that the message of the Lord spread rapidly. He is also asking that since we have heard the word of the Lord that we share the word of the Lord. We often get that confused and misunderstood, and we leave that part out. We want to make sure that the message of the Lord is spread through those who hear and do the word. We want to make sure that we give the type of credit we need to give by giving the Lord His due. When you spread the message of the Word of God, you are acknowledging that God's Word is true. You are exercising your faith by sharing this word of the Lord with persons who need to hear it. When you have been sent to share the Word, that will be the answer to exactly what they recently asked or what they stand in need of, you are going to be their vessel. And the rapidly is a sense of urgency. Are we sharing the word of God urgently, or are we sharing it like it is something that we can do at any time?

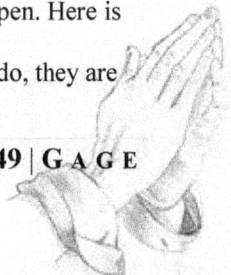

I am a previous retail manager. However, I hate to shop in stores. Going to the mall right now is just not my cup of tea. When I get into the store, I fix the displays, adjust the fixtures, criticize the customer service, and I am going to help other customers while I am there. I am going to resize the merchandise while I am in the building. Yes, that it is going to happen. Here is the problem with that. If I love store sales like some of my friends do, they are in love with sales, and they are in love with shopping. Now again, I do not like to shop in the mall. I did not say I do not like to shop. Shopping used to be my go to; I used to be addicted to the concept of shopping, however, understand these things. Number one, the Target ad. I used them specifically because they have dated ads. The sales start on Sunday, and it ends on Saturday. So if you know that the Macy's has a one-day sale which previews on Friday and the public sale is on Saturday. If you just saw something that was so dynamic, that was on sale or was so spectacular you are going to exercise a sense of urgency to spread rapidly that "good news." I put "good news" in quotation marks there because I need everybody to understand that is not the same Good News as the gospel of Jesus Christ; the Macy sales do not even pale in comparison.

So here is what we do know, let us see something that we just think is so dynamic and fantastic at the mall, we are going to use our cell phones. We are going to tweet. We are going to send it on Facebook. We are going to text message it. We are going to email it all at the same time. That was five methods of communication. Talking on the phone, texting, email, Twitter and Facebook. There are at least five more social media websites I can mention such as Vine, Pinterest, Flickr, Tumbler, and Instagram. Here is the issue with that though. When you were last at church, did you communicate the message in that same frequency with that same sense of urgency across all those mediums? And if the answer is no and you slightly dropped your head, I understand. Because Paul's prayer is still a standing prayer request, this is not antiquated nor is this old. This is still our charge that we go out and baptize them in the name of the Father, the Son, and the Holy Spirit, Matthew 28:19-20 the Great Commission. Here is our reminder: this is a standing prayer request.

You are the Word of God by reading this sermon, actively participating in church, going to Bible study, and your private study and meditation time. Do you understand the Word of God is the message of the Lord and is honored with you and is spread rapidly to you because somebody urgently shared the Word of God with you? Understand that is what we want you to do to others. This is a standing prayer request. This was not some 2000 years ago. Prayer is a daily activity. If you learned anything from this sermon, you are going to call, text, email, Instagram, Tweet, Facebook, Tumblr, Flickr, and any other social media or communication means. So we have a standing prayer request from a prayer warrior that requires our immediate attention. If this were an email, there would be a red explanation point, and this message would move up to the top of your list. Likewise with your voicemail, if you mark this message urgent, then this message electronically skips to the front of your messages in your inbox. This is what this means. Prayer needs to skip to the top of your list!

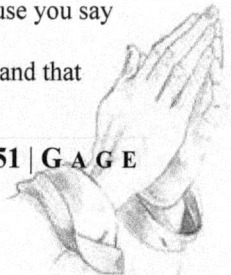

Verse 2 reads 'pray that we may be delivered from wicked and evil men for not everyone has faith.' Wicked and evil men do not have faith. I grant you that, but I want you to challenge in this area, some people are not wicked or evil, and they do not have faith either. And that is hard to say because you say ok that means that a Christian that I know that does not have faith, and that might be true. It is easy to say that is correct there is a Christian that you know that does not have faith. And all that is required is that we have faith of a mustard seed, and a mustard seed is quite tiny. And that faith of a mustard seed was paralleled and metaphorically designed to prevent the fact that they could multiply and that multiplication is an anomaly. You have got to multiply. So having said all that, understand that you have to say to yourself, self what do I need to do? To be able to move away from the wicked and evil ones, but that is not so much my prayer. My prayer is not to be the wicked and the evil one and that I have the faith that will please God,' Hebrews chapter 11 verse 6. You want to make sure that as we pray for the wicked and evil men, those are actual people you know. I said to someone the other day we talk about being delivered from satan, but do you realize satan shows up in people? The devil shows up in people! He does not show up transparently and say let me talk to you for a minute; I need to ruin your day for a little while. he shows up in people.

I am just going to drop a footnote right here, and you are going to think about this all day until tomorrow. he does not do that. he comes in the form of people you know and some you do not. satan is going to show up in your mother, in your father, in your wife, in your husband and your children. he is going to use those people, if he can. So my prayer is that we may be delivered from the wicked and the evil men, and not be one. I am just going to add that in there. I will not be that wicked and evil woman and that I exercise the appropriate measure of faith which pleases God.

Verse 3, 'but the Lord is faithful, and He will strengthen and protect you from the evil one.' The Lord is faithful. I was recently thinking about my situation: my financials, my career, my children, and I was thinking about my life overall. I thought about it, and I am in this place where I am uncomfortable. I am in this place where I am not happy. I am in this place where I am not getting what it is I would like and then I thought about it for just a second, a glimpse of my life passed by and then I saw that glimpse of others. I thought to myself this could be different and it could be by my definition definitely worse. Other people are dealing with situations that are so much more severe than mine. So I am careful to remember God's faithfulness in my life. I am careful to not misunderstand what it is that He has for me. And when I ask Him why do You have me in this place, why do You have me in this position right now, right here. Why am I here? I thought of a lot of reasons as to why. One of them is to give me time to focus on Him; it is to give me time to direct my energies toward Him. My situation is designed to give me time to be able to give to Him what time He properly deserves. As I give that some consideration, as I give that some thought, I have to ask myself if I were doing all the things I wanted to be doing, what time would I be able to offer to God, dedicate to God, commit to God, and to deliver to God? Would I be able to deliver the type of results that I am able to give Him now? I have to say probably not.

I have always been a committed Christian. I have always known there was a calling on my life. When I wrestled with my calling to preach in 1998, I immediately changed my focus in my writing career to make sure that everything was Christian based, and anything that was not representative of God, I would dismiss that from my publications. But five years later, God awakened me intentionally with a message of this is what I want you to do for Me: "I want you to preach the gospel and I want you to do it boldly, not parenthetically, stand outside those parentheses and outside the guidelines and outside of the boxes that are drawn for you. Stand on the other side of those lines and of those boundaries that are given to you because I have you." And God is faithful. He has had me from that day, before that day to this. He has had me every day of my life to this one that I am in today. He will strengthen you and protect you from the evil one.

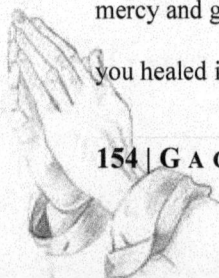

As you recall all of your life, you did not think is you were going to make it out of some things. You did not think that storm was going to end. You thought that category five hurricane was going to last the rest of your life, which your life outlasted that storm and that billion dollars worth of damage has been recovered and FEMA does not have you on delay and your insurance company did not fold. Your God, the Lord of your life, the God almighty, our Jesus Christ, the Holy Spirit is still right there, holding you, affirming you, enhancing you, encouraging you, delivering you from the evil and that is so limited to described what He has actually done. You were able to see God's hand, both mercy and grace. And you survived, and you had no idea that you would. And you healed in ways you thought you never would. And you can smile and hold your head up because God is there, and He is the strength in your jaw and your cheekbones to smile. And He is the prop under your chin so that your head is not at a 45-degree angle pointed due south. This is a standing prayer request. And a special prayer request by the prayer warrior, the intercessor himself.

Verse 4: 'Lord that you are doing and will continue to do the things we command.' Let us look at that pronoun 'we' for a moment. Now, we want to take Paul out of this for a moment and not misunderstand that Paul is not acting on his own accord. You know every word of the Bible is God breathed and all of God's word is useful for teaching and rebuking, instruction. We have to understand that 'we' command is from God. What Paul is telling us is straight from the Lord. It is not something that he made up because he wanted to. That is not possible. What Paul is sharing with us in this text and all of the books that he has written, all of the instructions that he gives, is not of himself. Lest I remind us that Paul never intended to preach the word of God. So when Paul says let us do it, I want to be first in line to say let us go because Paul is going to give you something to work with. Paul is going to give you something to do that is worthwhile.

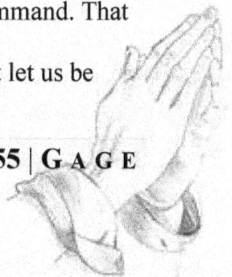

Paul is going to give you a God-sized challenge to change that is going to be so worthwhile and so valuable to your spirit. It is going to drive you to find those same opportunities again and again and again. So we have confidence in the Lord as you are doing and will continue to do the things we command. That you are doing. I am not going to get into an English lesson here but let us be clear 'you are doing' is a verb tense that is not active because the verb are is a form of the word be. And those are labeled typically as passive. You see, if Paul wanted to be active it should be that you praise and continue to pray that you serve, that you teach, that you worship, that you pray, that you honor, that you uplift, and that you bring God glory. Those are things that use active verbs, which require action, but he says 'you are doing.' We have confidence in the Lord that you are doing. Paul has traveled to these churches to give them the word of the Lord as directed by God. Paul has been directed to go certain places, do certain things, and find certain people. As is with the way, his ministry started.

With that being said, understand that we have to continue doing what we are assigned to do. Do not get confused by the verb command. We get all tightened up about that because it does not sound optional, it is something he is ordering me to do. He is a messenger of the Lord as are other people. As are other pastors and as are other ministers that you know. Let us keep in mind that we are to do the things that He commands because the rules are not any different for any other missionary of the Lord that the Lord has sent. Paul's words are not any different than that of David. Paul's words are not any different than that of Jesus. He is following what the Lord says. He is following. With that being said, we have to ask ourselves what do we do so that we can do what it is that is commanded of us and what happens when we have difficulties continuing to do those things which we are commanded. First of all, realize what you are supposed to be doing. Everyone's gifts are different. So find that out, what is your spiritual gift, and that can be done by spiritual inventory. But do what you are gifted at doing, it is what you will enjoy, and it is how you will serve without grievance.

Sometimes it is hard telling other people what to do because they want to say well who are you, you are not the boss of me and that is really sad. Because the idea is for people whose motives are pure and whose rights are relinquished. My pastor said that several years ago. And then God directed me to share some information with you. And I shared that information with you and I am maybe unknowingly completely how that fits your current world. You have to check the message and leave the messenger out of it. They are some unknowing individuals who have walked up to me and said things that are aligned with really the positivity of my spirit. They did not announce that the word of the Lord came to me to you through me. They did not do that. They walked up to me and have said some things to me, and those things were aligned with and in confirmation with what was already put in my spirit.

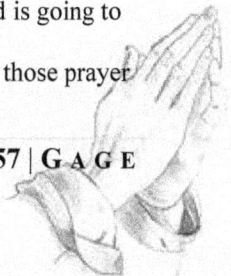

The Spirit is in people and those people are assigned to us; we are assigned to someone else. And what way we know is that we are to do something, and they may encourage us to continue to do some things or to introduce us to some new things that we are being designed for. And you have to be open with that because you do not know when and how the Lord is going to answer your prayers. You have some standing prayer requests, and those prayer requests are special to you. Likewise as they are special to you, you want those honors and sometimes He sends them through people so do not get tied up in the messenger and what the messenger says and manage to miss the message and delay your own blessing.

Verse 5: 'May the Lord direct your hearts into God's love and Christ's perseverance.' The scripture indicates two directions. I want my heart to follow those paths and be obedient to God's direction in these two directions. One, I want God's love in my heart. I want His love to override all of me. You know what happens when God's love overrides all of me and I cannot be persuaded to be a wicked and evil person that the devil wants to use to get someone else off of their walk for God. God's love will override all of me and heal me and bring me forward into His glorious wonders. The all of me. The all of me that only His love can settle down, calm and comfort—I want that.

I want love, God's love to take over my heart when I heal quickly. We talk about the fact that immune systems that heal quickly indicates that you are healthy and able to heal quickly from the hurts that come to you. That is your physical health though. We need to heal quickly with our emotions. When this occurs, it is because you have a healthy God relationship. You are healthy in your spirit. You can overcome some things very quickly. More quickly than previously. More quickly than others and more quickly than you even anticipated. And so I want God's love to take over my entire being. I want Him in my heart completely, bursting it wide open and all over me because there is not a part of me that wants to take on the devil's schemes. NO part of me that wants to submit myself to what the devil has planned for me. There are parts of me that can reject sin just at the view of it all.

And Christ's perseverance. In the garden of Gethsemane in Matthew 26, He asked this cup be taken from Him. If it is Your will, if not, then thine will be done. He has persevered through things when we would quit. He has walked in places, which we would just turn around and go the other direction. That is the perseverance that we want to serve the living God, our Christ, our Lord, our Redeemer, our Holy Spirit. For a standing request, a special prayer request from the prayer warrior himself.

Amen.

Lord God, how we love You and thank You for this day. Thank You for that word today. Thank You for replenishing my spirit through it Lord God. We thank You for that standing prayer request from a special prayer warrior. We thank You Lord God right now that You are there. That You cover us and keep us, keep your servants and our situation at all times. Lord God, we thank You right now for loving us the way You do. Lord help us better accept that love in the ways that it comes to us but sometimes it comes directly into our spirit. Sometimes it comes through the hands of others and lives of others. Sometimes Lord God, You just teach us how to love others so that we can be that person that love is repaid back to from the fullness of my spirit.

Amen.

Prayer: An Ongoing Assignment

1 Thessalonians 5:17 (NIV)

17 pray continually,

Lord God, we thank You for this day, for the ability to pray, for the power of prayer, and for the consistency of the Holy Spirit, Jesus and Yourself, in our prayers.

Lord, we thank You right now afresh for being God and God alone. For the purpose for which You have called us and the things that you have assigned us to Lord God. We thank You for those persons who have come into our midst whom we pray for. We thank You for allowing us to share with others what You give us to do in prayer.

And Lord, we thank You for the connection with the Holy Spirit that we will be able to pray to you fervently, and openly and honestly without stipulation or being stifled. So Lord God afresh, I thank You for what You are doing in our lives. Through Your son Jesus' name, we pray and ask His blessings. Amen.

PRAYER: AN ONGOING ASSIGNMENT

Pray continually is amongst what Paul has labeled as final instructions to the church at Thessalonica, and he gave them some things that they need to be doing. The instructions are in part: [16]"be joyful always; [17]pray continually; [18]give thanks in all circumstances for this is God's will for you in Christ Jesus." We need some context surrounding pray continually. Sometimes we pull verses out of context, and we leave them dangling because we do not give them any framework. The framework to pray continually is "be joyful always, pray continually, give thanks in all circumstances for this is God's will for you in Christ Jesus." Those three things are God's will for you in Christ Jesus so "pray continually for this is God's will for you in Christ Jesus" is not a contextually abused statement or rephrased or an edited version so for those grammarians that I travel with, I want to be clear that I fully intend to respect the text in its entirety and that is important because we want to understand the verse: "pray continually."

Now, I have mentioned this before but ten percent (10%) of 24 hours is 2 hours and 24 minutes. We want to ensure that we understand that 2 hours and 24 minutes of your day includes: prayer, study, meditation, our ministry to others, sharing your testimony, witnessing, and inviting someone to church. All those things are included in your 2 hours and 24 minutes of firm focus upon God. Prayer is among that 2 hours and 24 minutes; however, we need to ask ourselves "pray continually" means what? I always get asked this question: how am I supposed to pray all day? I am busy. I am at work. I am doing so much – how can I pray all day? Here is what that means: God wants prayer to be at the top of our minds. He wants it to be the first thing we do.

The first thing we do is pray because our prayer is communication and communion with Him; and so in your day in the things you do in the point that you might need carrying, in the fact that you may need a word, you need to be lifted, you need to be comforted. Prayer is the way and we want to give the time and to prayer because prayer is important. We want to make sure that we pray regularly, but regularly has a certain implication if we pray regularly – regularly could be once a month, once a year, once a week, once every other Thursday, that is a regular cycle but to "pray continually" means the daily moment to moment communication - so understand that praying continually means that it is a function of who you are.

You have to eat in order to live – it is proven, it is scientifically proven: you have to eat in order to live. Likewise, you have to pray in order to live. If you go without food for a certain period, then you will die; you will starve your body, and your body will no longer be able to function as it is designed. Your bodily organs will start to shut down. Can you live with that? Likewise, if you do not pray continually and regularly then your bodily functions: your mind, your spirit, your soul will start to malfunction and then you will die a spiritual death. While the spiritual death may not be as permanent as the physical death, it is still a death nonetheless and being that it is a death nonetheless, we want to consider how important prayer is to your continual regular diet of your life. So what do we mean when we say pray continually?

Do not procrastinate regarding prayer: "I will pray in a little while. I will pray after I am home. I will pray later. I do not really have time to pray." Honestly, if you do not have time to pray what do you have time to do? You are communicating with the most important entity, being, person, deity in your life. You see, we spend a lot of time with our cell phones, we hold it tight and we keep it close and we clutch it. We know where it is most, if not at all times. The first thing we do in the morning before we get out of bed and go to the rest room is that we touch that cell phone. We do something with it: text a friend, call a loved one; check our social media statuses; play a game, and sometimes we do all of this before we pray. We look at the time we spend with that phone and let us compare it to the time we spend with Christ, God and the Holy Spirit. We are coming up short – God is coming up short, and so are we for that matter. Our time with the Master, time with Christ, time with the Holy Spirit is coming up short. Now, do not procrastinate, do not put off the time that belongs to God.

We need to give God His time so He can give us what we need. You see, we want what we want when we want it, and we want it now. In that "newness," we have got to get to the point where we are going to give God that same "nowness" that we desire. Does He get that? No, we give Him the left over time, the time that is convenient, the time that gets in between appointment

A and appointment X. We do not give Him our first fruit, the first thing that happens when we wake up in the morning at His discretion. But we cannot procrastinate, we cannot put off the time that belongs to God, we need to stay focused on what belongs to God and how it is we can best give Him that without Him having to prompt us to get our attention or even to appear that He is begging. We want to be sure that we do not procrastinate – what time do we give to God in prayer? As you continue to build your prayer life, you are going to crave that time. You are going to be in a funk until you can get back to God and pray.

That is a function also of praying continually: do not put your prayers in a box. What I mean by that is realizing that praying continually does not require going into your prayer closet as described in early scripture. Sometimes you have to pray in the boardroom right before you start to speak and to present and ask for those contracts and build those relationships. You have to pray before you go into your office and before you leave your office because you do not know what you are up against in your corporate world or your classroom or your playground or your mall or wherever you serve. You have to pray when you get into your car: The Lord allows us to make it from A to our destination, B. You might want to give God His prayer time. Now, you can be proactive or you can be reactive but praying continually will equip you to go into scenarios without anxiety, without pressure, with His peace that only He can give which transcends our complete understanding. Our prayer reaffirms our faith. Our prayer lets the Holy Spirit know I need your comforting right now so while we want to avoid prayer or limit God through our prayer: where we pray, how we pray, what position or posture in which we pray. I do still believe we should kneel, and I am personally working on kneeling, however do not get paralyzed by that. I am good at praying on the go. I am good at just praying in the middle of my thoughts. The Holy Spirit just drops a footnote and anchor right there which prompts me to stop whatever it was I was thinking about and/or doing and pray right then: "Lord God our Father afresh I thank You on this day." Do not forget that we are praying to God because He is our Father.

For those of us who have a human father present, if you all have such relationship you know there is not a day that goes by that you do not talk to your father. As we grow older and older we appreciate those relationships more and more because somewhere somehow a bell has gone off in our heads that says these are some of the last few days of this person's life and you learn to appreciate fathers that much more because you are in a position to understand their worth and you too are on a different playing field now – you are not 8 years old, neither are you 21 anymore but you are at an age where you appreciating the things that you heard them tell you, and things they told you to do. Now, you communicate with them differently. The same concept applies with our God our Father; I want to hear from Him, so I urgently seek Him. I crave our time together. I cannot wait to hear all He says next.

Do not overrate the length of prayer. We think that if we have a long prayer that God will be impressed - that may not necessarily be the case. You see we do not have a lot of time to pray. When you pray, you pray authentically and you can just pack it in, get straight to the point there is nothing flowery around it then you will be able to say: "I just gave God what He wants of me, no fluff, just prayer, just me."

As you pray continually, do not forget to pray the scripture. As we bring God glory and build our relationship and our prayer life, do not forget that the Lord wants His word right back. It is a profound experience when I pray, and I open my prayer with a Psalm. Psalm chapter 8, verse 1 says: "Oh Lord, our Lord, how excellent is thy name in all the earth." As I recite in that scripture as I'm praying, my voice is going to drop, my eyes are going to close, and I approach the personal space with just God and I in it. And if I do not say anything else but "thank You," that is enough because I have given over to Him my heart at that time. I have shut the whole world out right there when I say, "Oh Lord, our Lord, how excellent is thy name in all the earth." Maybe you have to see it or hear it to understand it but when you say those scriptures and you understand those words, you will get the meaning.

Do you believe that which you speak and pray? There is nothing that can stop you from what happens next. As you pray continually, do not forget to leave room for God and the Holy Spirit. Do not be so quick to hop up and say "amen" and run off to the next thing. Give the Lord some time and if He says nothing, just sit there and feel the Holy Spirit. Do not be so quick to run off, "Ok God I prayed and I have other things to do." Where are you going? What do you have to do? I know that the calendar is packed fully: I am the best one I know at double booking, overbooking, and entirely booking my days, the weeks, the months and years. I know but our Lord and Savior, our Lord, His Father, and our gift, the Holy Spirit, deserve as much of your time as anybody else. As a matter of fact, they deserve more.

Do not be perfunctory in your prayers. There are things that we do in a pattern; there are things that we do in a specific way; there are things that we do differently; yes there are. However, we want to be sure that we do not get patterned in our prayers so that they sound the same, and they lack authenticity. Our prayer would then lack our heart's connection—that is what we do not want. We want to get to a point where we can say beyond the shadow of a doubt that I prayed specifically and fervently to the Lord today. Likewise, we want to give God who we are – our true self. Do not allow yourself to get into the routine of what you say to God. I know there are people who have a standard opening: "Our God, Our eternal God, afresh we thank You" – yes, sometimes I say that. However, their prayer also sounds the same. It sounds scripted. It sounds as if they have written their prayer, and that is all they know to pray. It is almost like they pray The Lord's Prayer. There are some standard movements in their prayer and in that we can get complacent, and we can lose our authenticity, we can stop having a heart connection with God, and that is not uplifting. We want to get into a position where we can say to God, "I just want to give myself to you in prayer, there is a place where I want to give myself to you – and we want to be able to do that – we want to get to that level where we pray that way, not because of performance but because of relationship. Prayer is based on relationship. The more time you spend, the more time you'll want to spend. The more time you spend, the more authentic you'll be. The more time you spend, the more you'll want to share. Your guard will come down, and you will be able to give of yourself in a different manner. You will fervently seek Him like you never have before, and you will share your prayer life with others.

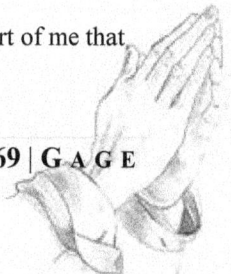

Share your prayer life with others. Do not neglect to do those things that will allow people to get a glimpse of your prayer life. I used to pray over my children when they were sleeping because that is when I could get them still. When my daughter, who is the older of the two wants to hear me pray out loud, I pray in her presence; I pray in her space, and I hold her hand when I pray. The people who love us and who are intimate with us need to see and hear us pray. When she hears me pray, I am sharing God with her. Prayer is a part of me that only few people are exposed to, and I do not wear the mask in front of God. I do not wear a mask for her, so she has heard me cry when I pray. She has heard me tell the truth in prayer. She had gotten answers to questions she did not have before she sought the answers, and she got that revealed in prayer. And so those are the times when you are the most open. Fort Knox is down, and you can be your true self in prayer, and there are persons around you who need you to reveal that to them. They do not get you; they don't understand you, and they don't know why, they don't get it, but prayer will be the start of that knowledge. Some people are very selfish about their prayer time, that much I understand. However, if they are important, if they are special, if they're going to be lifelong partners in your life – a spouse, a lifelong spouse, your children or your best friends, those are people who should know what your prayer life looks like. They should not be confused at all. They should not be concerned. Also, they should not be clueless. They should know that this is how she prays! This is what happens when she prays. I recently published a book of prayers and journals, and I opened it up with a dedication that says (and I paraphrase in my own words):

This book is dedicated to those of you, who hear me pray, know why I pray. This book is dedicated to those of you who make me pray, hear me when I pray, understand why I weep when I pray, understand why others weep when I pray, understand when you can't hear me when I pray and understand why – others who make me accountable to prayer… and that is my dedication.

Do not forget that this prayer time is not your grocery list and your wish list. It is not a time when you tell God all the things that you want material wise. This is a time to ask for forgiveness for sins; this is the time to ask for help and heal and to be healed. This is a time when you share your burdens with the Lord because He says that He will bear them for you. This is the time when you share your battles or potential things you're going to have to fight so that you can give it over to him. He can fight your battles so you can be still. This is the time when you share with Him the real hurt. This is when you tell Him I have not forgiven this person – help me forgive to person. This is when you bare your soul. This is where you admit it to yourself. This is where you share it with Him. When you are going to share with God, you say those words out loud and that makes it real and that calls you into action. You cannot stay in the same position and not be called into action when you say those words out loud, there is no way! Do not forget that you will hear from God during this time and every time. Hear from God in this prayer time – be careful to listen for Him. Do not forget that prayer is really making yourself available to God to hear from Him and for Him to hear from you. Sometimes He just wants to know how you are going to tell me what I already know. It is similar to when I ask my child a question, "Did you do that?" It is not a rhetorical question. It is not a trick question. I just want to know that you are going tell the truth.

Pray continually.

Pray without ceasing.

Have an attitude of prayer.

Amen!

Lord God, Afresh we thank you for this time, this vessel, this message.

Thank you for working on our hearts, our spirits, our minds, our souls through these lessons in prayer. These series Lord have been simply profound. And Father God, thank You for that! We thank You for all You are doing in my life personally, and I thank You by extension for all that You are doing for other persons who are present in this show. Lord, I thank You for those whose lives are blessed. Thank you for sharing that blessing with me on yesterday.

Lord God, I thank You right now for the travelling mercies You offer each of us each day. And we thank You for the relationship that You allow us. We thank You for being available to us, and we thank You for the gift of our intercessor and our Lord and Savior, Jesus Christ. It is in His name that I ask these blessings, and I pray this prayer. Amen.

The Prayer of Encouragement

1 Corinthians 1:4-9 (NIV)

Thanksgiving

4 I always thank my God for you because of his grace given you in Christ
Jesus. 5 For in him you have been enriched in every way—with all kinds of
speech and with all knowledge— 6 God thus confirming our testimony about
Christ among you. 7 Therefore you do not lack any spiritual gift as you eagerly
wait for our Lord Jesus Christ to be revealed. 8 He will also keep you firm to the
end, so that you will be blameless on the day of our Lord Jesus Christ. 9 God is
faithful, who has called you into fellowship with his Son, Jesus Christ our Lord.

Lord God how we bless You and love You and thank You on this day; And Lord God, I thank You right now because You are able to cover us, keep us, keep us healthy and available unto Yourself. Lord God, we thank You for putting us into communion with Your Holy Spirit and Your Son Jesus Christ, Lord so we may be fulfilled and be participants in Your covenant

Lord God, we thank You right now for being faithful to Your work, keeping Your own promises which are something that we find so sparingly, and so rarely these days.

Lord God, afresh I thank You for being God and God alone for all the things that You do and all that You are, all that You cover us with and keep us from, Lord I thank You right now.

Lord I thank You for this day that You do for us exactly what You wish that we would do for each other and ourselves. It is in your Son Jesus' name

that I ask for Your forgiveness of our sins; through your Son Jesus' name we pray with blessings.

Amen.

The Prayer of Encouragement

As we consider these scriptures, we want to remind ourselves and for those of us who do not know: Paul is blessed with his ability to pray. Inside of the words he has authored inspired by God, he prays and he prays with the fervency and the zeal to give you some understanding of Christ. In this empowerment, he empowers you to pray, and he encourages you to pray. The prayer of encouragement from Paul is nothing new, and there are several prayers that he prayed that would be defined as the prayers of encouragement. As a servant of the Lord, Paul was gifted to encourage us through prayer. We want to make sure we always understand that we have to take our own advice: take advice from people who are servants of the Lord. Be very leery of people who walk up to you, give you advice, and they don't walk the walk that you walk. Be very careful of people who tell you they have your best interest in mind, but they don't walk the walk. It is very difficult to have someone share with you, and they do not walk the walk – be very leery – be very concerned with that. In this life as a Christian, fellow Christians should be able to walk the walk.

As a person who may be seeking a deeper prayer life, please take advice from someone who has an active prayer life. I want someone who relates to what I am going through and my prayer life is similar. I want to pray with someone with a greater or similar prayer life. That brings us to Paul; Paul's life is a mark of excellence regarding how he came to Christ, what he was doing before he came to Christ and his immediate obedience – he did only what it is that Christ called for him to do. Not many of us could say that, not many of us could tell that story – not with truthfulness anyway.

So, verse 5 says, "for in Him you have been enriched in every way, in all your speaking and in all your knowledge." When we consider the gifts God gives us, when we consider the things that God puts before us, we have to give consideration to the fact that the Lord gave us these gifts to use for Him. It is not something that he gave us just because he thought a lot of us. God gave us these things because He needs us to do something for Him. As Paul prayed for you, he encourages you yet he reminds you, yet in this reminder, I want to share, the thing he gives us the most of is being able to know that God still has His eye on us, that He has not lost sight of us, that He has not forgotten us.

Verse 5 also reminds us that it's because of Him that we have these gifts and privileges. He gives us the credit for being able to articulate our train of thoughts, through speech as well as the knowledge to do so well, but He reminds us that it is because of Him for in Him you have being, not because of yourself but "for in Him."

Verse 6 is the finishing of that sentence "because our testimony by Christ was confirmed in you." We could see our testimony within your body – within your body of believers – within your church – within your body of believers we can see Jesus Christ confirmed, we can see the testimony. Now, this is a report, this is the first one and so this is very important to this for he wants to keep them going.

Verse 7 – "therefore you do not lack any spiritual gift as you eagerly wait our Lord Jesus Christ to be revealed." You have everything you need. The Christ gave you the gift that is why you articulate so well, and you have everything you need. When Paul tells that he had everything he needs, one of the things he was saying was: stop fretting, stop worrying, stop complaining, stop searching. Isn't that what we do? We have a plate full yet we still want to know why we don't have macaroni and cheese or why we don't have green beans or where is the cornbread; we're always looking for something additional without being satisfied with what is on our plate. We've got to be satisfied with what's right here. Otherwise, there is no possible way for us to get this accomplished – no possible way.

We spend our time as Christians always second guessing what we have in front of us, what we have inside of us, what our calling is, what it is we should be doing, who we should be helping, whom we should serve, who should lead us and where we should go. We spend all our time as Christians doing just that. That can be a bit cumbersome, not to mention discouraging and not to mention against God's will. We have to stop second guessing. That is one of the reasons why Paul encourages us – verse 8 "He will keep you strong to the end so you will be blameless on the day of our Lord Jesus Christ." Right there we want to be focused on the fact that He makes us strong. He is in charge of our strength. He undergirds us with His power. He gives us that freely because of the will – because of His will and what He has gifted us for. You have got to ask yourself, "How do I get to this point? How do I get to this level?" Well, I am in a position to accept the encouragement from Paul and the strength from Christ without complaint and without issue. It becomes critical that we start to follow through without complaint and issue. If we do not accept the encouragement, then we do not have the opportunity to be all that God plans for us to be, we do not have it. We are going to miss something—something important. We are not going to be in our proper place if we fail at this mark. We cannot be out of position for the work that God has for us. When we're out of position, when we are not in place, when we are not doing something, we delay our blessings and the blessings of someone else as well as. We delay our blessings severely. In our severe delay, we can set God's plan back, we can delay what is planned for us. We cannot deny God's plan; that is not possible, but we can delay it for sure. We should not have the opportunity to delay God's

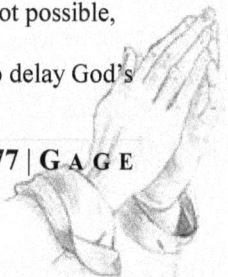

plan. We do not have time to delay God's plan. We all stand in desire of God's blessings. Why would we delay His blessings in that manner?

Let us talk about the reason Paul would encourage you and consequently why we should encourage one another, why we should refer ourselves to these types of scriptures. Verse 8 "He will keep you strong to the end so you will be blameless on the day of our Lord Jesus Christ." "He will keep you strong to the end…" I want to refer us back to that great character in the old testament in the book of Job. Job is a character who was strong in the Lord, he was an upright and righteous man, he was doing exactly what the Lord had asked and directed him to do; he could do nothing wrong. The Lord could find no fault with him, was seeking no fault in him, understood no fault to be with him and overall was just pleased to have Job as a servant. Now, I want to let us be clear about the fact that while that was the case, the devil was looking around for something to do. And mind you, the devil is not a dumb individual, a dumb entity, nor a dumb spirit; he's absolutely not but what he is a person – the devil is a person who can say such things as: "Do I have permission to sift your servant?" God can say "yes" or "no" and that is what happens: either you are sifted or not. The devil asked for permission to sift Peter and Jesus said, "I'm praying for you." But he asked for permission, and God said, "His soul belongs to me, but you can do what you wish with whatever else he's got." There's a limit on what He allows the devil to do and what the devil has access to – there's a limit. So even with such as request, he has limited powers granted by God. Now, inside of that we want to understand that Job's situation was one that was rather unique. It was rather unique because for 42 chapters Job has an outstanding experience. For 39 of the chapters, he and his friends talked but God never said a word. Technically, nobody encouraged Job in that walk and Job encountered some terrible things: he had his children taken away from him, he had a wife that kind of a little leery and a little wary about what to do. But all in all, Job's story is designed to encourage you. If you have never read the book of Job, just read a little bit of it and get in the first couple of chapters what takes place and line up your story- lay it side by side; parallel it and compare it if you will but understand this, everybody has a story. Just because you do not know it does not mean there is not one there. It is our job, by design per scripture that we are to encourage one another, uplift one another, provide for one another, and when we're not doing those things, we fall short. We fall short in a fashion that was not by design but our own doing. You can find someone to encourage and you can authentically encourage them. It does not take anything away from you. You are not going to lose anything by encouraging another person. If you are doing your job as a Christian, when a member distances themselves, we should have reached out further. If you have that perception that someone has moved the response is not, "Well, you know, whenever she gets ready to come back, we'll be right here" – no! You go to that person, and you seek to help them because if we do not our behavior is the trick of the enemy. You see

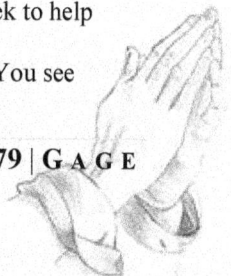

someone pull away, and you let them go off by themselves—that is not what we are supposed to do for one another.

So you may give people an understanding of who you are, but when you need to encourage them it doesn't matter who they are. It does not matter who they are to you. It does not matter what they do, call and encourage them. Paul encourages each of us because it is the will of God – because it is the will of God that we do so. So, God will keep you strong until the end, if you don't read the meat of the message, chapters 3 – 39, and you just pick up at the end ,chapters 40 – 42, you will see that Job was strong to the end. During that time of his issues – during that time, God said nothing but Job never blamed God. Job never cursed God. Job never hated God. Job never questioned where God was. Job had trouble with his circumstances, but he never put himself in a position where he acted as if God was common. He never acted as if God just had abandoned him. God will keep you strong to the end.

We go through things on purpose. The things that happen to us are done purposely. There is a trust that is given over to us when we go through stuff and that trust is given to us uniquely so we can continue to be trusted by the Lord and inside of that trust He needs to know we can persevere through some things. It does not say that we are not going to go through some things but that we will be strong to the end. A part of that being strong to the end is being able to pray and have others intercede on your behalf and to also encourage you.

So the proper thing to do is to say: "Onedia, I missed you. I haven't heard from you. I haven't seen you. You are not participating at a level where I am accustomed to seeing you normally participate."

Our design is to remain encouraged through the whole trial and test process. So Paul's job is to encourage us. The part about being blameless is a little tricky. As we talk about being blameless that we understand that a being, Job, was a great example of this. Be sure in your trials you do not sin, and you are not reckless against God. You want to ensure that you are not reckless against a God who created you, whom you serve, who gives you life's breath, who gives you gifts, who gives you the ability to do all the things that you do. That is what being blameless means because you will not be without sin, you will not be without fault but the blameless piece is to ensure that you do not sin against God in that category and making sure that you are not encroaching on things that do not pertain to you.

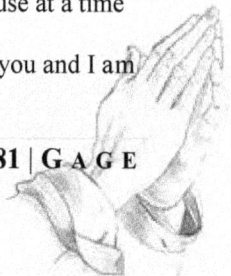

It opens to that part about me asking God, "Why me?" but what happens when God replies, "Why not you, Onedia, why not you? You are strong and very courageous as it says in Joshua, so why not you? You are bold enough to ask me for some things that are visibly impossible, David – why not you? I give you things I do not give anyone else – why not you? I know you are disappointed. I know you are in pain – but why not you? Because at a time when I can trust you to remember that I have My hand underneath you and I am holding you where I have you, and I am protecting you in that place. I may let the devourer approach you, but I do not let the devourer have you." God is faithful, and that is enough said. It is the prayer of encouragement that empowers us and reminds of who we are, why we are, where we are and what we ought to do in the process; and remember a call that each of us has is to encourage one another.

Amen.

Lord God, afresh we thank You this day for what You've done in our lives; for who You've put in our paths and for the calling You have on our lives; for everything you want us to do dear God, we thank You. We praise You. We lift Your Holy name on high, Lord God, and we share with others with an uncompromised boldness that only You can provide and be the source of. We thank You right now for being able to serve You all of my life, being able to be undergirded by the Holy Spirit, being able to do exactly what it is that You have for me to do. It is in Your Son Jesus' name that I pray and ask all these blessings. Amen.

Prayer Between Wisdom and Revelation

Ephesians 1:15-23 (NIV)

Thanksgiving and Prayer

[15] For this reason, ever since I heard about your faith in the Lord Jesus and your
love for all God's people, [16] I have not stopped giving thanks for
you, remembering you in my prayers. [17] I keep asking that the God of our Lord
Jesus Christ, the glorious Father, may give you the Spirit of wisdom and
revelation, so that you may know him better. [18] I pray that the eyes of your heart
may be enlightened in order that you may know the hope to which he has
called you, the riches of his glorious inheritance in his holy people, [19] and his
incomparably great power for us who believe. That power is the same as the
mighty strength [20] he exerted when he raised Christ from the dead and seated
him at his right hand in the heavenly realms, [21] far above all rule and authority,
power and dominion, and every name that is invoked, not only in the present age
but also in the one to come. [22] And God placed all things under his feet and
appointed him to be head over everything for the church, [23] which is his
body, the fullness of him who fills everything in every way.

Lord God, afresh we thank You, for You said in Your due time You will reveal all things and in all wisdom, and if we lack wisdom we should just simply ask because You regard wisdom and the first sign of wisdom is the fear of the Lord. So Lord God right now, we thank You for doing exactly what it is You do inside of us, in our lives, in our midst and what You show us which is to give you glory. Lord, we thank You right now because You are God and God alone, and in all of that Lord God, we thank You for being able to seek You fervently. So, Lord God, I thank You right now because of who You are and what You do in my life, and I thank You for using me as Your vessel to deliver Your word. It is in Your Son Jesus' name that I pray and ask these blessings.

Amen.

PRAYER BETWEEN WISDOM AND REVELATION

I love Paul, and Ephesians is my very favorite book of the Bible. I love Paul because he is considerably authentic and considerate of whom we are as people. I want you to understand that there's a reason why Paul is who he is, understand the inside of the prayers that he prays, understand the discussions that we have around prayer, understand why so many of his discussions relate to prayer, and understand that Paul has many reasons to pray. When we talk about this prayer between wisdom and revelation, we want to understand what our role is in prayer and who we are.

We want to talk from the perspective that there are some things that we are supposed to know. Our prayer time needs to be consumed with the need to know some things. Our prayer time is designed to reveal information to us. In verse 17, he says, "…may give you the spirit of wisdom and revelation so that you may know Him better." He is preparing to share the wisdom and revelation.

Wisdom and revelation already have to be evident to know that you do not know. There is an adage in the work environment, in the corporate world, that says "you don't know what you don't know" and then there is this other cliché that says "ignorance is bliss." What we find in both of those statements is that there is truth, and then there is some conflict of interest. You see, in our grand world where we are that we think is so fabulous on earth there is a quest for knowledge, and then there are those people who just do not care. They have no care in the world regarding the knowledge that they are supposed to have. Then one day you realize that there is knowledge that you do not have which is when you realize that you do not know what you do not know. When you are learning new information, there should be a seeking of knowledge, there should be a quest for knowledge, there should be an aspiration for knowledge, but again, you do not know what you do not know. And what you will have to figure out is that "how can I find out what I do not know?" In order to realize that there are things you do not know and to start to seek some things specifically that you do not know and to be able to find the source of those things that you do not know, requires considerable wisdom.

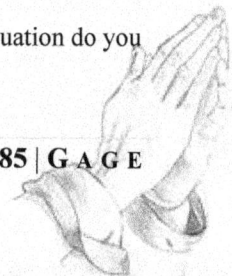

Now, we talk about wisdom which typically is to find out something that gives us experience matched with the ability to know - and it is not something you can see on a person, something you can hear from him and something you can feel, but wisdom guides you in making some different choices. Wisdom allows you to be silent in the room when you really want to speak but know it is not prudent to do so. Wisdom is when you can sit and look at a situation, assess that situation and decide, discern from that situation do you really want to be bothered with that whole situation. Wisdom is when you become a grandparent, and you share things with your grandchild that you wish someone had shared with you. Wisdom is doing those things. Wisdom is investing in the life of another when you are not going to get anything in return. All those things are based on wisdom. We need to mature so that we can put ourselves in a position where we can base our behavior on wisdom.

There is a scripture that states you need "a council of advisors" so who is going to be this council of advisors? Who is on your council of advisors? What do you want a council of advisors to do in your life? How do you accumulate a council of advisors, and if that wisdom is, having a council of advisors, who do you talk to? Who shares wisdom and who reveals things to you between wisdom and revelation? And as you look at wisdom and revelation not as a destination but as a journey and on a continuum, you will need to grow wiser and to have more revealed to you as a process of that revelation every day. What is it that they offer to you? Wisdom is not always older. As we grow up, we need to be conscious of the fact that wisdom is not always older. We really want to be clear since wisdom is not always older, making sure that you do not fall into that category. You do not want to fall into the category of being a dumb, old person. That should be part of your prayer, "Lord, allow me not to be a stupid, old person." For as many days as we spend on this earth and as many of those days that we have been walking with the Lord, evidence of that every day walk should be some wisdom, should be some knowledge of Jesus Christ but that wisdom should allow you to respond and act a certain way and without that wisdom, we have been labeled a fool. Because we have avoided wisdom, we have not sought after it. We have not asked for it, and we have not used what we thought we had. We cannot neglect wisdom and its value.

So as Paul prays about the wisdom and revelation that we may know Jesus better, there needs to be enough wisdom and revelation already present to know we do not know Him well enough and then it should inspire a craving within us to seek and seek more of Him. And it also should inspire an urgency within us, a calling on our lives, an appointment, an anointing to pursue Him and show Him to others. Now, one of the things we will have to do is being able to ask ourselves is 'where am I on this continuum of wisdom and revelation?' Where are we? If you should label yourself between one and ten on wisdom, how wise are you? I would say I was a five, but I also have to say to myself do I have a complete council of advisors? And the answer is no. I do not have a complete council of advisors, but why is that?

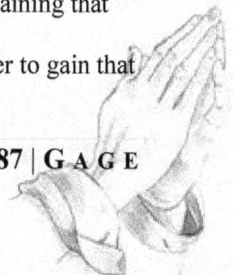

So we do not have a complete council of advisors. Who are those persons? Are we praying for these persons and their timely arrival? And your advisors are not going to stay the same all the time; however, I personally still do not have a full council of advisors. We have to be focused on gaining that wisdom. We have got to be focused on what God has for us in order to gain that wisdom. We have got to put ourselves in a position and a posture where we can receive wisdom. We also need to be judicious of the wisdom at the level that we are supposed to because wise persons do not handle wisdom foolishly. We need to seek that wisdom; it is what God expects of us. We need to seek opportunities to use the wisdom we have. When we consider the fact that our wisdom is what separates us from other believers and definitely non-believers, we have to decide how we are going to move forward with what we have, who we know, what we know and what we come to be about.

Our wisdom is also going to be related to our calling. God gives us wisdom as it relates to what it is He has for us to do. Wisdom also means that we have to be on the alert at all times. We have to be available all the time: mentally, spiritually, and emotionally. We have to be available at all times and wisdom is required to do that.

Now, we spend a lot of time on that because it is very critical. Verse 19 says "that power is like the working of His mighty strength which He exerted in Christ when He raised Him from the dead and seated Him at the right hand of the heavenly realm over all rule and authority power and dominion and every title that can be given not only in the present age but in the one to come." That is how much power He has. I like how Paul says that God exerted His power. Paul frames what is important for us.

If you indeed have an area where you can exert some power and authority, might and strength then what you feel is that you have influence. If you are going to exert that influence, you should think about exerting that power that needs to be in the best possible place. In our personal lives, what is the best possible place to exert the power that is given to us by God? Is it the gossip at the beauty salon? Is it to start mess in the church? Is it that you are simply cantankerous because you are an old person but not wise? Is that the place to exert that type of power or strength or might? Absolutely not, that is a shabby exhibit of what Christ has given to you to use or the reason He died for us to be able to have that. That is an exceptionally poor exercise, an exceptionally poor exercise. There is a reason He gives us what He gives us, and it is to give Him glory, so when you ask yourself on what should I use this might, strength, power and influence? You should use the might, strength and power at places that give God glory, because if God does not get anything out of this but grief then the answer is no then we want to be sure to click the bypass button, the excuse me button, put up your Baptist finger and tip out of the conversation or the situation when our wisdom is tested. I know that is difficult because before we know it, we have let the devil use us and put himself in a position that we are compromised, and we have sacrificed our relationship with God. We look up and find ourselves unable to walk away from foolishness. We really do; we find ourselves unable to walk away for some foolishness that could easily be avoided by just simply saying "no, thank you." We have got to get to a place where we behave better than that, we have got to get to a place and we understand that our hearts and minds and our souls are to be pointed towards Him.

Verse 18 "I pray also that the eyes of your heart may be enlightened in order that you may know the hope for which He's called you to riches of His glorious inheritance in the saints and His incomparably great power to us who believe." The word enlighten means to impart knowledge, to instruct. It is about spiritual information too. We are in a position right now where that becomes critical. We cannot have one more incident where the Lord says, "I want your heart and all of its contents. Point it towards Me," and we tell Him to wait! We expect Him to wait. We need to reach the point where we do not say to Him "wait." We are working to say to Him, "Here is my heart as an offering." However, we cannot offer our hearts to God because they are dirty.

The reason Paul prays that the eyes of our heart may be enlightened is so we that can have an awareness to know how to clean it up, to ask for the Lord's help in cleaning it up and being able to move away from those things that make our hearts horrible. You see, some of us do not know that we have a dirty heart.

We have to ask ourselves: "Do I have the best intentions for those who come into my presence, or am I always looking for something that is for me?" Am I always looking for the blessings, wishing it was for me, and I never consider that it should just be about somebody else from time to time? I was recently put in a situation where I needed some help from someone and they did not give it to me and I was put back in the position of needing some help and this time they helped me but would I have been in a different situation had they helped me the first time? The answer is likely to be yes. I sometimes wonder if because the first time the person was stingy that I was put in that position again so that they had to help me when I asked the second time but over a period of time, the money given ended up being the same. It was interesting to look at that from that perspective because I always wondered when He says that He will make it happen; it is always interesting to me how does He make it happen. And do you realize that that is happening at that time from a previous occasion.

From wisdom to revelation we have to be wise in order to carry out His desires and His need for us, we have got to be able to be revealed to, we have got to be knowledgeable enough to know that we need affirmation. We have to do those things; that is why our prayer life while seeking Him is very critical and important. Amen.

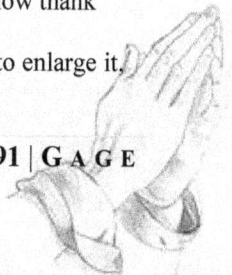

Lord God, afresh we thank You for wisdom. Lord, I ask You right now for more wisdom and more revelation. I thank You right now for using me as Your vessel, trusting me that I will articulate Your word as long as You give it to me, that I will rightly divide the word of God and hand it over as instruction for those around me, those who come into my path. O Lord, right now thank You for the territory that You have given me, and if You see need to enlarge it,

Prayer Between Wisdom and Revelation

Lord, I pray for the wisdom to understand my role in that enlargement. I thank You right now for the vision You give me for my life, for showing me what is going to happen next. Thank You for that revelation; and Lord God, I thank You right now for this audience that they may be enlightened, that they may be considered wise, that they may come into a better knowledge and understanding of You, Lord God. I thank you right now for the forgiveness of my sins. Thank You for me being able to walk in your righteousness that You may add all things after we seek Your righteousness.

In your Son Jesus' name, we pray and ask these blessings.

Amen.

Resources

www.onediagage.com

www.bible.cc

www.lifeway.com

www.biblegateway.com

They Like to Never Quit Praising God by Frank Thomas

The Homiletical Plot by Eugene L. Lowry

Celebration and Experience in Preaching by Henry H. Mitchell

The Certain Sound of the Trumpet by Samuel Proctor

360 Degree Preaching by Michael J. Quicke

Expository Preaching by Haddon Robinson

The In Between Times by Ralph D. West, Sr.

The Four Pages of the Sermon by Paul Scott Wilson

Acknowledgements

God, thank You for Your plans for me. Thank You for ***With An Anointed Voice: The Power of Prayer*** and choosing me to complete Your project. I just want to please You. Thank You for continuing to anoint me and to invest in me and my gifts, which keep surprising me. Thank You for loving and forgiving me.

Hillary and Nehemiah, thank you for supporting me and my endeavors. Thank you for loving me, especially when I do nothing without a pen and a clipboard, thank you for enduring my late nights, your ideas, the sounding board, the love and the support. Thank you for celebrating our legacy.

Kimberly 'Ann' Joiner, thank you for reading my work and offering your honest feedback. May your life be blessed by me doing God's will.

To my prayer partners and to my accountability partners, thank you for the long talks and the powerful prayers and the encouragement. To my pastor and church family, thank you so much for your love and support.

Acknowledgments

Minister Onedia N. Gage seeks to share her outlandish pursuit of God with her prayers, study and meditation. She desires to share her faith in a manner which helps you do the same through her calling. She hopes that these words bless you.

Please feel free to contact and share your testimony.
onediagage@onediagage.com, or @onediangage (twitter). www.onediagage.com

Blogtalkradio.com/onediagage

Youtube.com/onediagage

Facebook.com/onedia-gage-ministries

PREACHER ♦ PRAYER WARRIOR ♦ TEACHER

To invite Rev. Gage to preach, teach, and pray, Please contact us at

@onediangage (twitter) ♦ onediagage@onediagage.com ♦ facebook.com/onediagage

youtube.com/onediagage ♦ blogtalkradio.com/onediagage ♦ www.onediagage.com

www.ingramcontent.com/pod-product-compliance
Lightning Source LLC
Chambersburg PA
CBHW022128080426
42734CB00006B/277

* 9 7 8 1 9 3 9 1 1 9 4 5 2 *